ANN M.
MARTIN

ANN M. MARTIN

by Margot Becker R.
with Ann M. Martin

SCHOLASTIC INC.
New York Toronto London Auckland Sydney

ISBN 0-590-45877-9

12 11 10 9 8 7 6 5 4 3 2 1   3 4 5 6 7 8/9

Printed in the U.S.A.   40

First Scholastic printing, April 1993

Many thanks to all the people who openly and generously agreed to be interviewed for this book. Thanks also to the dozens of people who put time and meticulous effort into editing and production. And thanks, of course, to Ann Martin.

Contents

1
The Diaper Years

Ann Matthews Martin was born on August 12, 1955. Hurricane Connie was whipping through the little suburban town of Princeton, New Jersey. Rain soaked the maple trees and flowers on the lawn outside the Martins' apartment. Ann's parents piled into their Chevrolet station wagon and drove the few blocks to Princeton Hospital. About five hours later, Ann was born. Her father, a cartoonist, joked that they ought to name the baby Connie Gale, after the storm.

Mr. and Mrs. Martin chose the name Ann instead. They wanted to call their child something simple, so other kids couldn't tease her about her name when she got older. Her middle name, Matthews, is her mother's maiden name (her mother's last name before she married Ann's father — in those days, all women took their husbands' last names).

Ann was the biggest baby in the hospital — eight pounds, two ounces. That may not sound so big today, but babies are born larger now because we know more about nutrition and pregnancy care. The nurses nicknamed her "The Eight-Pounder." She was born with dark brown hair. It later turned blonde, almost white.

After a few days at the hospital, the Martin parents took their new daughter home. They had a little two-bedroom apartment, which they shared with their cat, Tigger. (Recognize that name, Baby-sitters Club fans?) Ann's father, Hank, had been using the second bedroom as his artist's studio. A few months earlier, he had rented another studio downtown, and he and Ann's mother turned the empty room into a little nursery. They went to a secondhand store and bought a crib, a rocking chair (which they've saved to this day), and a kitchen table, which they covered with a mattress pad and made into a diaper changing table.

Things were a little different back then. For instance, there were no throwaway diapers. Ann's parents used cloth diapers. We had a president named Eisenhower. Marilyn Monroe was talking to the press about doing a TV show. A computer was as big as a whole room! A newspaper cost just five cents.

Before Ann was born, her mother, a teacher, had quit her job in order to devote herself to her child. Of course, these days, many women continue to work either part- or full-time after they have a child. But back in 1955, almost no one did.

While her husband worked hard all day in his studio, Edie Martin took her new baby for walks in the carriage. They met up with other mothers and small children. Most of the fathers were off at work in New York City. The mothers watched the kids play in their yards or in the playground a few streets away. Strangers would stop Edie Martin on the street and coo at the baby. Ann was chubby, with little blonde curls. Someone told Edie the baby should be a model, but the Martins wouldn't consider it.

When Ann was born, her grandparents bought the family their first television set. Can you imagine the Martin parents not owning a TV until they were thirty? But it was pretty normal then. TV was new, and not everyone had one. Ann's father held her on his lap and they watched *I Love Lucy* for the first time. Maybe that's one reason Ann became such a devoted Lucy fan.

Princeton was a good place to grow up then, and it still is. It's quiet and safe. Princeton's curving, tree- and flower-lined streets give it a relaxed, country feel. There are a lot of interesting lectures and art events at Princeton University, which is one of the best colleges in the United States. Princeton also has a regional theater, an art museum, and a few great libraries. It's only an hour or so from New York City, too.

Princeton kids can play outside, explore the woods around the houses, and ride their bicycles

Ann playing dress-up, at two in 1957

into the center of town. In its own way, Princeton has it all.

When Ann was two, her parents began looking for a house to buy. They wanted a place where they could put down roots as the family grew. They moved to a small gray house on a dead-end road while they looked for the right home to buy. The house had a big screened-in porch, and the family would eat out there in the summer. Ann had one of her very first birthday parties on it.

The big news around that time was that Ann's sister, Jane, was born. When the Martins brought the new baby home from the hospital, Ann's mother knelt down on the ground outside the house and opened her arms for Ann to come and give her a hug. Ann ran toward her . . . and right past her to where her father was standing, holding Jane. She was fascinated by the baby then, and remained fascinated with children as she grew older.

Raising a family was difficult in those years. Hank Martin was struggling to make a living as a cartoonist and artist. Each day, he rose early in the morning and went to his studio. The tiny converted tailor's shop on Charlton Street looked almost like a large dollhouse. When Ann was a little older, she made a set of white, blue, and raspberry red curtains for the studio, and they hang there to this day.

It was fun watching Dad work. Unlike her friends, Ann could really *see* what her father did. He would come home at night and show Ann

1959 — Ann at four with her father

sketches and finished cartoons. Sometimes he would work at home. Ann would peer over his shoulder and watch.

Henry Martin did as much artwork as possible. He painted a huge mural of a fruit basket on the wall of a kitchen supply store. He put some giant painted flowers on a neighbor's tennis backboard. Ann and Jane were proud every time they passed something their father had created. Later on, a famous literary magazine, *The New Yorker*, began publishing Mr. Martin's cartoons, and he became well known for them.

Ann's father felt lucky that he could leave his office at six each evening and be home by 6:15. The Martins were able to sit down together for dinner at 6:30. Ann would play with Tigger and Kiki, the Martins' two cats, under the table.

The Martins were big cat lovers. They got Tigger when the woman next door brought home a stray and the Martin parents fell in love with him. Tigger lived to the ripe old age of seventeen. By that time, he was lame, and the Martins carried him up and down the stairs. (By the way, Kiki got his name because that was the way Ann pronounced "kitty" when she was small.)

At one time, the Martins actually had *nine* cats. They'd had five, and then one had kittens. And yes, all those cats actually lived *inside* with the Martins. Over the years, the Martins' cats have also included Sweetheart, Fluffy, Jerry (who followed Ann home from the school bus stop in sixth grade), Pumpkin (whom Ann's mother found sit-

Ann on Pets

"I think one reason people like to have pets is because we want to have something to take care of, something we're responsible for. That's one of the very first ways we learn responsibility. My family *always* had pets when I was growing up. In addition to the cats, we had hamsters, mice, turtles, guinea pigs, and fish.

"I like cats because they're so responsive. Cats think of things themselves. A gerbil probably isn't going to try to figure out how to get hold of the pen you're writing with. Cats definitely have their own opinions. And they have senses of humor. Certainly, my cats make me laugh, and I'm pretty sure that sometimes they do it on purpose. I think they know when they're being funny and even when they have an audience. Also, they're very affectionate, which is nice. There's something comforting about waking up and finding a cat right next to your head!"

ting on a shovel in a puddle of mud), Honey, and BJ. BJ moved over from the house next door on his own. No, the neighbors didn't accuse Ann's family of cat-napping. They celebrated the move with a toast.

Ann was already shy and quiet at this young age. In fact, her Aunt Adele (Ann's father's younger sister) thinks Ann was just born naturally shy. She says, "Ann was a listener from the very beginning. She had a good attention span at a very early age. She always learned so much from listening — and still does. If adults were gathered, she'd be sitting there not bothering a soul, but she was taking in every single thing that was said."

But Ann was also prone to nightmares. She says she was afraid of everything — monsters in the closet, being left alone, sleeping in the dark. She thought foxes lived under her bed. She slept with the overhead light on — a night-light just wasn't good enough. Maybe this is why Ann became somewhat of a homebody. She liked sticking around the house, where she knew all the kids and where her mother or another helpful adult was always just one shout away.

But Ann's fearfulness should not be mistaken for weakness. She is capable and determined, with an iron will to get things done. Says her childhood friend, Beth, "She was extremely disciplined and self-motivated. It allowed her to accomplish everything she is now. She had a vision that let her look at a long term project and do all the things she'd actually need to finish it." Ann had an intensity that wasn't obvious from the outside.

A few years later, Ann's Brownie troop leader wrote in her autograph book at the end of the school year, "Quiet, serious, dependable Ann. You'll go far if anyone can." You bet she would!

2
Family

The Martins took their responsibilities as parents very seriously. They planned their lives around their children. Mary B. Rice-Whittemore, a close friend of the Martins during the years when Ann was growing up, describes them by saying, "Edie's real outgoing and Hank is kind of low-key. They're very family-oriented and they doted on their girls in the nicest kind of way. Ann had a very solid family, very supportive and caring. There was a lot of good humor, too."

Hank Martin came to Princeton as a young man to attend the university. He fell in love with the town and stayed on. He hadn't met Ann's mother, Edie, yet. She was living in Illinois and working as a nursery school teacher. But Edie's brother, Rick Matthews, *was* living in Princeton. He was a librarian at Princeton University.

In 1952, tragedy struck Edie and Rick Matthews's family. Their younger brother, Stephen, died suddenly. The Matthews parents wanted to get away from home, which reminded them of the tragedy. They moved north to Princeton to be near their son, Rick, and stayed in a beautiful boardinghouse near the downtown area while they looked for a house or apartment to move into. It just so happened that Hank Martin was living in the boardinghouse at the same time. The Matthews parents became friendly with him. When their daughter, Edie, came to Princeton for a visit, they arranged for her to meet him. Hank and Edie hit it off famously, and were married a year later. Two years after that, Ann came along. Jane arrived in two more years.

Ann at eight posing with her family

The Martins always kept in close touch with the rest of their family. Though none of Ann and Jane's grandparents lived in Princeton, they were very close with the girls. They visited often, and the Martins traveled to see them as well. Ann was still on a bottle when the Martins flew to Kentucky to visit her father's parents for her very first Christmas celebration.

Hank Martin's father would have been any kid's perfect grandfather. Grandpoppy knew just how to play with kids. He'd get down on his hands and knees on the carpet and start a wild game of horsey with his granddaughters. He was almost completely bald, but he let the girls tie ribbons in the few, wispy strands of hair he had left.

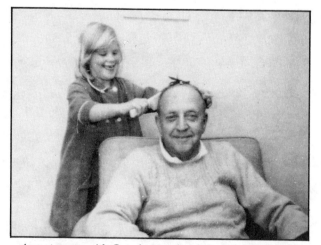

Ann at seven with Grandpoppy, her father's father. He was endlessly playful and good-natured.

Grandpoppy had a large collection of windup toys. They included a Frankenstein monster whose face turned red when his pants fell down. There was also a bear who fished and a rabbit who read a book. The girls thought this was amazing — a grown-up who loved toys.

Ann had a very special relationship with her father's mother. Granny really appreciated Ann, and tried to draw her out of her shell. Aunt Adele says, "My mother loved people, and people loved her. You just never went anywhere — to the dry cleaners or the drugstore or wherever — without her making friends. Granny was very outgoing and had a wonderful laugh. She was warm, definitely an extrovert. Ann probably was very taken with how Granny could be that relaxed and giggly, and how she could reach out to all sorts of people so easily. Granny was always laughing, and made you feel like a million dollars."

Ann and Granny would snuggle up quietly together on the couch while the other kids ran around the house playing and getting into mischief. Granny taught Ann to knit at the age of eight. (Her mother had taught her to needlepoint the year before that.) When Ann was older and began writing poetry, she'd always send Granny copies. She dedicated her first book, *Bummer Summer*, to her.

Granny had a very special doll, called Jane, which she had played with herself when she was a little girl. Granny gave Jane to Ann when Ann was ten. Ann renamed the doll Amelia Jane. She

In 1964 Ann was nine, and Amelia Jane was already over sixty years old.

wanted to keep the Jane part for Granny's sake, but she'd just read a biography of the first woman airplane pilot, Amelia Earhart, and she desperately wanted a doll named after her. Ann treasured Amelia Jane. Many years later, in the spirit of tradition, which is so important to her, she passed Amelia Jane on to her cousin, Aunt Adele's daughter Margaret. Today, Amelia Jane is almost one hundred years old. She sits in a special place in Aunt Adele's room.

Granny lived to a very old age, and that's why Ann got to know her better than her other grandparents. Ann was thirty-two when Granny died at the age of ninety-four. Ann was saddened, confused, and overwhelmed. Granny's death sparked the idea for the book *Claudia and the Sad Good-bye*.

Ann used many of her own feelings to describe Claudia's reaction when Mimi died.

The Martins kept in close contact by phone with Aunt Adele and Uncle Lyman (Ann's father's older brother). They both lived in Kentucky with their families. Today, Ann remains very close to Aunt Adele. Adele is a warm, well-spoken woman with a soft Southern accent. She and her husband Paul work tirelessly through their church to help people who are sick, poor, or face discrimination. She is also a committed needlepointer and seamstress, like Ann. They talk a lot over the telephone about clothes they're sewing or embroidery projects they're completing.

Aunt Adele describes her relationship with Ann by saying, "I don't feel the age difference between us. I think if I really had a problem, I could go and talk to Ann — not just as my niece but as a person who would listen and be understanding."

Uncle Lyman had a great sense of humor and wrote Ann and Jane long, funny letters. Ann used to love visiting his family because he and his wife had kids who were older than she was. They were Louise and the twin boys, Lyman and Jimmy. Ann was thrilled to hang around with *real teenagers*. They listened to rock and roll, and Louise had boyfriends, and everything. Plus, the family had a dog, which was exciting and fun for confirmed cat owners like Ann's family.

Ann also saw a lot of the other side of her family. After her mother's parents left Princeton and moved to Florida, they stayed for a few days with the Martins every time they made the trip from Winter Park, where they spent the winters, to Maine, where they spent the summers. Ann and Jane always looked forward to the gifts they'd bring. Ann still remembers the Chatty Cathy doll they once brought her.

Ann called her maternal grandmother Neena. Neena loved music. She wasn't a professional musician, but she sang in the church choir, and studied the piano for many years. In fact, she continued to take lessons well into her seventies! She loved opera music, and would listen to it on the radio as she polished the silver and did other house chores. Her life revolved around her church. She instilled a strong sense of duty and volunteer spirit in her daughter, Edie, who passed it on to Ann and Jane. Ann says, "One of the reasons I was close to Neena was because she was very involved in family, and she had researched our family tree. She always had fascinating stories about our ancestors."

Grandpa gave the appearance of being stern, but he really wasn't. Grandpa was an avid sportsman. In college, he had run track and played baseball. He loved going to the Princeton University football field to watch practice. Jane says, "I could always get a baseball mitt out of him every time we visited, because I was such a tomboy. Until our cousin Peter came along, I was like the grandson he didn't have." But Grandpa was a voracious reader, too, like Ann. They both always had their noses in a book.

Edie's brother, Rick, and his wife, Merlena, lived nearby to the Martins. They baby-sat for the girls often, especially during the time Ann's father was sick in the hospital when Ann was five. Uncle Rick and Aunt Merl would take the kids to the zoo or the shore, while Ann's mother was visiting at the hospital. Uncle Rick would also take Ann to watch the crew races on Lake Carnegie in the spring. They'd root for the Princeton University team, of course! He was great to be silly with. He played with the girls as if he were a big kid himself.

Aunt Merlena was very artistic. She'd teach Ann to sew puppets or Barbie clothes. She used to help make Ann's party invitations and helped out at Ann's first few birthday parties, too. Aunt Merl was great with kids, Ann reports. She'd tell everyone to pretend to be elephants and other circus animals.

Both Rick and Merlena are librarians. Rick isn't a professional author, but he loves to write. Their house was filled with books, like Ann's own home. Says Ann, "Wherever we went, we found ourselves in a house full of books."

Ann's ancestors were real old-time Americans. Her mother's family came here on the *Mayflower*, over three hundred years ago. They settled in the Connecticut area. Ann's father's family came soon after that, from England. They moved to Connecticut also. A hundred years later, their descendents helped to start a little town called Peacham in Vermont. The town didn't exist before Ann's ancestors and a few others actually built it! That side of the family eventually moved to Kentucky, where Mr. Martin and his brother and sister grew up.

Ann says, "Family — and I don't mean just the immediate family, but family in general — is important to me. Jewelry, furniture, photos, anything that's handed down in the family becomes extremely important to me just because it's part of the family."

It has always been important to Ann to stay close with her relatives. And when she makes good friends, they become as close to her as family, as well.

The Ring — A True Family Story from Ann

"My great-uncle — my grandfather's brother — was a newspaper reporter during World War I. He got tuberculosis and went to a sanitarium in the mountains while he was sick. He fell in love with and became engaged to his nurse, Rosalie Cross. And he gave her an engagement ring that had been in our family.

"But my great-uncle died before they could marry. Still, Rosalie wore the ring all her life. She never married.

"She stayed in touch with our family. I met her once. When she died, she willed the ring back into our family. She wanted to give it to 'Henry Martin's eldest living daughter,' which was me. So I have the ring. It's very important to me. It's one of my most treasured possessions just because it's in the family."

3
Sisters

There couldn't be two sisters more different than Ann and Jane. While Ann liked dressing up and sewing, Jane was a tomboy. While Ann cared most about doing well at schoolwork, Jane concentrated on extracurricular activities. While Ann played and worked mostly on her own, Jane did best in groups. While Ann was quiet and retiring, Jane was active and bouncy.

They even look different. Both are blonde and pretty, but Ann is medium height and thin, with sharp, delicate features. Jane is six feet tall (she says she's 5′ 12″), and has a curvy figure, and rounder features.

Back then, though, Ann was much bigger and heavier than Jane. Her fat period lasted from second through fourth grades. (If you know Ann now, it's hard to believe she *ever* had a fat period.) Jane didn't grow tall until she was a sophomore in high school. For a long time, she was tiny. (This is also hard for people to believe who know Jane as an adult.)

Of course, the girls did an awful lot of playing together. Their favorite childhood game was Baby. Ann would be the mother, and Jane would be the child. Ann would feed Jane a bottle, or they'd make a crib by pulling the pillows off the couch and standing them up to form the sides. Then Ann would make Jane take a nap.

Both Ann and Jane had special blankets. Ann's was named the Mommy Blanket and Jane's was called Tickly. They still have the blankets stashed away. They couldn't bear to throw them out.

The girls had a few different playhouses and tree

Ann, Jane, and Fluffy in the backyard at Dodds Lane. Ann's blanket is in her lap.

houses, which they built with their parents' help. The first of these was a dollhouse made from a big cardboard carton which the cats took over. A little later came the playhouse in the Martins' backyard. Ann dared to sleep in it all night once — alone. The last was a tree house in the woods behind the house. There's a big story about the tree house later.

Dress up was a favorite game for Ann and Jane. They had a huge yellow trunk packed with old clothes, hats, shoes, gloves, and costumes. It was just a secondhand wooden trunk, but their dad had painted scenes from *Winnie the Pooh* on it. The girls would put on makeup, and Mr. and Mrs. Martin would take movies of them. They'd put on their favorite outfits and create entire plays around

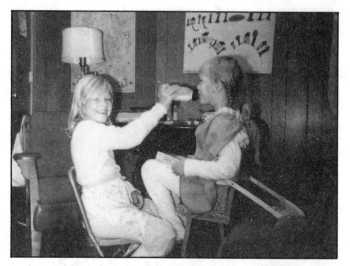

Ann and Jane playing one of their many games of ''Baby'' in the house on Dodds Lane.

them. The sisters shared an incredible make-believe world.

Ann and Jane also liked to set up stands and outdoor stores. They had a few lemonade stands. About three or four motorists would stop and buy a cup. They also sold their old toys and comic books. Or they'd pick wildflowers or strawberries in the field behind the house and sell them to passersby. Every so often, they'd hold a Dodds Lane carnival. They would charge a small fee for a chance to play ringtoss, spin and win, or balloon burst. A carnival just like Ann and Jane's appears in Ann's book, *Inside Out*, and in the Baby-sitters Little Sister book *Karen's Carnival*.

The Martin girls never made too much money from their stands and events. After they earned back the money it cost to buy lemons and sugar, they only had a tiny bit left over as profit. One year they planned a big event so that they could buy their parents an anniversary present. But they cleared only seven dollars! And that was doing well! Sometimes they didn't even break even. But mostly they had fun, so the projects were worth it.

The girls took many different types of lessons after school. Art was one of Ann's favorites. She also loved her horseback riding lessons. Other classes Ann took were ballet, ballroom dancing (her least favorite class), piano, and guitar (briefly). She enjoyed learning new things and did well with all her lessons.

Ann on Art

"Art is a wonderful way for kids to learn to express themselves. Through their creativity, they gain self-esteem. They can prove to themselves how much they can do if they hold up a painting and say, 'Look, I did this.' And dance is similar. It's very important for kids. These are things they can do fairly easily. And they're fun."

Jane took art and especially loved her acting classes. She refused to go to the ballroom dancing classes — instead, she played cards behind the couch in the coatroom. She was on the soccer and lacrosse teams at school. That couldn't have been more different than Ann, who hated gym and had a terrible case of stage fright.

Like all sisters, there were times when Ann and Jane were jealous of each other. Ann often wished she were more outgoing and social, like Jane. Jane sometimes envied the excellent grades Ann always got. But Jane says she didn't compete over school with Ann.

Jane describes it by saying, "Ann would always come home and just be by herself. She'd do her homework and get A's. I would cut class, run to the pizza place with my friends, come in at five, watch the *Flintstones*, do a half hour of homework, and get on the phone. We were always just totally different."

One of the reasons Jane had trouble in school was because she was dyslexic. That means she sometimes saw letters and numbers backward. A *b* might look like a *d* to her, or she might read the word *pot* as *top*. This did not mean Jane was dumb — far from it. But it did make reading and arithmetic very hard for her. Reading just wasn't fun for Jane the way it was for Ann. Once the Martins discovered the problem, they took Jane to many different doctors and specialists. Now, Jane really enjoys reading, but she's still slow at it. Some Baby-sitters Club fans believe Claudia is dyslexic, and that's why she has trouble in school herself. Ann thinks this is probably a good theory. Ann wrote about a dyslexic girl and her sister in the book, *Yours Turly, Shirley*.

Ann and Jane were very different kinds of kids, with very different abilities. Luckily, their parents knew how to appreciate each child for what she did best.

As Ann grew older, she began to be a bit embarrassed when her little sister would tag along after her. She wasn't necessarily the kind of person who'd get mad and blow up, though. If she and Jane had an argument, she'd give her sister the silent treatment. Then Ann and Jane would make their parents give each other messages for them — even if they were in the same room. They always made up later.

Today, Ann and Jane are close. They share a few

friends, and enjoy having dinners together, or catching a movie. They both work very hard, so when they can't get together, they have long talks on the phone.

Ann says, "Jane and I used to be just sisters. Now, we're best friends, too."

The sisters grown-up

4
Dodds Lane

When Ann was four and Jane was two, the Martins bought three quarters of an acre of land on Dodds Lane. They watched their new home go up from the first shovel of dirt for the basement to the last nail on the roof.

Over the years, the Martins decorated the house with wooden furniture, upholstered chairs, and photos of the family. On cold days, a fire crackled in the living room fireplace. Portraits of Ann and Jane hung in the dining room. In the rec room, Mr. and Mrs. Martin filled two yellow cabinets with art supplies — pastels, crayons, paints, paper, material, felt, paste. Anything the girls might need for an art project was probably in there.

Ann had her own room. Her mother helped her hang up drawings she'd made in nursery school, and there was always a shelf full of picture books. As she grew up, Ann changed her old bunk beds (which she'd used for sleepovers) for twin beds. The baby drawings were replaced by peace posters (which were a big fad in the sixties) and a photo of Bill Cosby. And Ann collected figures of horses, and almost a full set of Nancy Drew and Bobbsey Twins books on her shelves.

Their first year in the new house, the Martins had a small Christmas tree in a pot — roots and all. They planted it on the front lawn after the holidays, and eventually it towered over the house. The London plane trees and ashes also grew tall. Mr. Martin, an avid gardener, planted beds of tulips, azaleas, and daffodils, as well as a vegetable garden in the backyard, with beans, tomatoes, and other good things. The kids would pitch in. They liked planting seeds and just generally getting dirty.

Ann and Jane (in the middle), and friends selling wild strawberries at a sidewalk stand. That's the Dodds Lane house in the background.

Ducks and geese flew overhead. Deer wandered through the woods. The Martins hung a hammock in their yard. It was perfect for swinging in while reading or petting the cats.

The neighborhood grew around the Martins. New houses were built. The street was lengthened. Sidewalks were put in. By the time the six nearest houses were finished, seventeen kids were living in them! The kids were all ages and had different personalities, but they played together.

The cast of characters included Beth McKeever, five houses up from the Martins. Beth was Ann's best friend and her partner in just about everything. Susie Valentine — energetic, lively, and a few years older than Ann — lived across the street with her three brothers and sisters. Two houses away were the Rices. Ann baby-sat for Robert (known as Bo then), Carl, and Molly Rice for many years. Mike and Kappy Meyers lived next door with their dog, Pepper.

Ann describes Dodds Lane by saying, "I was one of the older kids in the neighborhood. It seemed like there was always some group of younger kids to organize and play with or take care of." In fact, the way the kids played together on Dodds Lane has an awful lot to do with how things are set up in Ann's books.

Though the imaginary world of Stoneybrook, Connecticut, isn't an exact copy of Dodds Lane, the *feeling* of the two places is very similar. In both, many different types of children play together. Their interests connect at times, but there are al-

Ann with two of the Rice kids (her most frequent baby-sitting charges), and other Dodds Lane friends. Carl Rice is on the far left. Molly is in front of Ann.

ways a few separate activities going on. Problems may occur, but people support each other when they do — like the time a little girl from Dodds Lane got lost and the whole neighborhood went looking for her.

The kids played on the sidewalks, in the backyards, and in the field and woods behind the houses. They'd wander down to Harry's Brook to catch minnows (nobody knows who Harry was). They might play on the Martins' slide and swing set, or hit a tennis ball against the Rices' backboard. A favorite Dodds Lane game was Empire Tag. The person who was "It" would hide, and everyone else had to seek. When you found the hiding place, you got in, too. The last person to find the spot had to be "It" next.

In the winter, the best sledding route was down the hill on the Martins' front lawn, across the snow-filled street, and up the lawn of the Valentines' house across the way. The kids made dozens of snow forts, snowmen, and snow angels.

There wasn't much traffic. When cars did come by, they drove slowly. That was thanks to Ann's mother, and a few other parents, who asked for a twenty-five mile per hour speed limit on Dodds Lane. The kids got around by foot, bike, skateboards, roller skates, or a combination of the four.

The adults on Dodds Lane had many friends on the street, too. The Martins were close with the Rices and the Valentines. People knew their neighbors well, and counted on each other.

Dodds Lane was very comfortable for Ann. She knew all the kids, and liked most of them. Yet when she'd had enough activities, she could always go to her room, close the door, and shut out the world. Her room was a magical little kingdom for her. There, she could read books, do art projects, or finish up a needlepoint piece. She might invent an imaginary world, peopling it with her stuffed animals. She actually enjoyed being sent to her room so she could make up stories and plays. Of course, this skill of creating an imaginary world was something Ann would use when she became a writer.

Even homework could be fun. Ann enjoyed concentrating and doing her work well. She never had any trouble entertaining herself in her room. There was always something to do.

5
Best Friends

Ann's best friend, Beth McKeever, lived a few houses away on Dodds Lane. It was great having her right there to share secrets with, dream up imaginary worlds, and play games. Beth was the only other girl Ann's age who lived nearby, and they quickly became as close as sisters. Beth says, "Ann was just always there for me, and I was always there for her."

Beth was a lot more physical than Ann. She was almost a year older and a few inches taller. She had thick brown hair, which Ann envied because her own is fine and thin. Beth was active and energetic, funny and adventurous. Ann looked up to her because Beth wasn't shy. She was always doing something, going somewhere, and being part of everything that happened at school and around Dodds Lane. Beth was a pacesetter. She

Ann and Beth — best friends in eighth grade . . .
and in twelfth grade.

was the first female captain of the patrols in the elementary school. As an adult, she would become the first female firefighter in her local volunteer squad.

Beth describes the differences between her and her best friend by saying, "I was the one who would try to sew a dress and it would end up rolled up in the closet on the floor. I thought that was a fine place for it to be. Ann would stay up and make the dress work, and make it fit . . . and it would look great!"

And Beth adds, "I think there were probably times all through our growing up that I wished I could have been a little bit more like Ann and Ann wished she could have been a little bit more like me."

The character of Kristy was based partly on Beth. Actually, Kristy is a *heightened* version of Beth. If Beth liked sports, Kristy loves them. If Beth was a little outgoing and energetic, Kristy is a lot that way. Writers often use this technique — they take an idea or a character from real life and exaggerate it. Because of the way Ann exaggerated Beth's character, Kristy seems sort of overbearing and bossy and Beth wasn't.

One of Ann and Beth's favorite games was secret agents. They'd spy — mostly on Beth's mother — and talk to each other on pretend walkie-talkies made out of bottle caps nailed to blocks of wood. Another special game happened at Beth's house during twilight. The goal was to run from one set of bushes across the lawn to the other bushes without getting lit up by the headlights of passing cars.

The girls also played Employment Office. In that game, they pretended one of them was an office manager and the other was every single job applicant who walked through the door. The applicant would put on different costumes and take on various characters for each person who came in. The girls were serious about the game. They even made up a questionnaire that the applicants had to fill out.

Actually, this game isn't too different from Let's All Come In, which Karen Brewer makes up in the Little Sister books. Karen and her friends pretend to run a hotel, and each person is one of the new guests. In fact, Ann's father was *really* the one who played that game. Aunt Adele was the littlest one, so she always got stuck with the worst parts. Sometimes, she even had to play a dog!

Ann's driveway was paved and on a hill, and made for great daredevil skateboarding. It also became a drawing surface for intricate chalk creations. When the weather was hot, Mom or Dad would drive the girls to the Princeton pool for a swim, or they'd take a dip in a friend's pool. (That family also had a trampoline!)

For Halloween, Ann and Beth often created a spook house in Ann's basement, with sticky, goopy spaghetti for ghost insides and peeled grapes for eyeballs. They also tied long threads from the pipes overhead, which felt like cobwebs when you walked through them with your eyes closed. Each year, they made a tape recording of scary sounds. Ann always got to do the scream!

When the weather turned cold, the girls would go skating on Lake Carnegie. One time, Ann and Beth brought out a hockey puck. They were determined to play just like the boys. But they had no idea what they were doing. They didn't even know the rules! Even so, they carefully taped up the handles of their hockey sticks, because they'd seen other kids doing it. They had a great time falling all over the ice and laughing.

When it rained, the woods behind the houses on Dodds Lane would sometimes fill with water. If there was a cold snap and the water froze, Ann and Beth would pull out their ice skates and glide around among the trees. It was a special feeling, sort of magical. It was very different than zipping along on the open space of Lake Carnegie.

In the spring, a favorite activity was riding around on Beth's family's lawn mower. Back then, those weren't very common, and everyone wanted a chance to drive it. (They were only allowed to do so when Beth's father was around.)

While Beth was busy cutting the grass, Ann was busy planting flowers. She loved gardening. She enjoyed taking care of the mountain pinks, tulips, daffodils, and crocuses.

Sleepovers were a must. It was fun snuggling up under the covers, talking about friends and classes, or inventing secret codes together. Ann loved the book *The Secret Language*, by Ursula Nordstrom. And much later she wrote a book about a different kind of language herself. It's called *Jessi's Secret Language*.

Ann and Beth did a lot of silly things together. Once, they exchanged hamsters. It didn't seem to matter all that much — both hamsters did their share of lying around, nibbling food, and trying to get out of their cages. One of Ann's hamsters, by the way, was named Frodo, after the beloved character in J.R.R. Tolkien's *The Hobbit*. Baby-sitters Club fans will recognize that name from the Pikes' hamster in Ann's books.

Ann and Beth had their share of clubs. Usually, they were Beth's idea (just like the Baby-sitters Club was Kristy's idea). But the clubs never worked out nearly as well as the Baby-sitters Club does. Ann and Beth would get a group of girls together at one of their houses on, say, a Tuesday afternoon. But they'd never quite know what to do. They'd play for a while and then go home. None of the clubs lasted more than a few weeks.

For a short time, Ann and Beth belonged to the Pussy Cat Club. But the club didn't really have anything to do with cats. In fact, Beth didn't even own any cats! A few years ago, Ann decide to write a Little Sister story called *Karen's Kittycat Club*. She liked the name of her and Beth's old club, but frankly, she couldn't remember exactly what it had been set up to do. So she made up a completely new idea.

Most of all, the girls used to start Projects with a capital *P*. Ann and Beth fed off each other's energy. One of them would come up with an idea, then the other would think of a good way to start it. They'd egg each other on until a large-scale project actually got finished.

They'd write plays and put them on, create all the scenery and play all the parts. That meant madly changing costumes "backstage" (upstairs in the hallway above the living room or in the kitchen or dining room) for every new character that appeared. Music was sometimes a part of the plays. The girls would bang around on the piano and make up songs.

For many years, a Christmas time production of Charles Dickens's *A Christmas Carol* — starring Ann, Beth, and Jane — was a tradition. The girls would invite their parents. Sometimes Beth's parents couldn't make the "opening night" performance, so the girls would take the show "on the road." They'd move everything up the street to Beth's house.

Once, the girls put on a circus in Ann's garage. They made signs and invited all the kids on Dodds Lane. They set up chairs and charged a quarter for admission. The problem was, they hadn't really planned what they'd do once everyone was assembled! They tried to pull handkerchiefs out of a trick magic container that looked empty, but it didn't really work. They had a few tightrope walking acts and tumbling acts, but those were short. After about twelve minutes, they took their bows and said good-bye. (Things don't always work out as well as they do in books.)

Another project was the library that Ann, Beth,

and Jane set up in Ann's room. They pasted pockets with cards in the backs of their books, and let the kids from Dodds Lane check them out. There were late fines and everything. The library also featured an exhibit of insects the girls had caught, pinned onto a Styrofoam board, and labeled. (Ann's pretty grossed out by bugs now, though). Later on, the library idea appeared in Ann's book, *Inside Out*, and in one of the Baby-sitters Club books.

For a few months in sixth grade, Ann "published" a newspaper, with help from Beth. She'd collect Dodds Lane news — such as if someone got over a bad case of the flu, or won a contest, or earned an award in school, or even something sort of dumb, such as if someone had been waiting for a mail order toy for a long time, and it finally came! Ann wrote the paper out in longhand, in columns. Back then, Xerox machines were hard to find, so Ann piled up a few sheets of paper with carbon paper in between. She'd give the paper to five or six families on the street.

Ann included contests in the newspaper — things like "make the best drawing" or "write the best story." It was a job with a lot of deadlines, a lot of repetitive hard work, and a lot of writing — not too different from the work she does now with the Baby-sitters Club!

Ann and Beth's friendship remained strong over the years. There were times when they were more close and times when they were less close. They each had other friends. But they were always there for each other. When they went off to different colleges, they kept in touch by letter. They looked forward to vacations, when they could see each other again. They'd talk for hours then, to make up for lost time.

Beth got married when she was twenty-one and Ann was her maid of honor. Beth's married name is Perkins. She has three daughters, Myriah, Gabrielle Ann (Gabbie), and Laura. (Yes, Gabbie's middle name is in honor of Ann.)

That's right Baby-sitters Club fans, this is the *real* Perkins family. Beth sometimes talks to kids she sees reading the Baby-sitters Club books and tells them she knows the author. Not only that, she tells them the Perkins girls are based on her kids. And even more, she is the real live Kristy. Most

The best friends as adults. Ann poses with Beth and her growing family in 1985. From left to right are Beth's husband Eric, Myriah at age four, Ann, Beth, and Gabbie who had recently celebrated her first birthday. Laura would be born two years later.

of the time the kids don't believe her!

Ann has become very close with Beth's daughters. They talk on the phone a few times a month. Sometimes, the family will come into New York City and Ann will go with them to a show, restaurant, or museum. Recently, they went to the American Museum of Natural History, which has a lot of animal displays and dinosaur bones, and they renamed it the Museum of Dead, Stuffed Things.

A few years ago, Ann and Beth celebrated thirty years of friendship. Ann gave Beth a handmade collage with memorabilia and photos of things they'd done together over the years. Beth says about Ann, "She's so reliable. She's my comfort zone. Whatever happens, I know I'll get back on an even keel when we talk to each other. Everything comes into balance again."

Ann on Friendship

"Probably one of the most important things in life, and also one of the most difficult things to find, is friendship. I mean *true* friendship. Loyalty is one of the bases of a solid friendship, that's for sure. Without it, a friendship isn't going to last long.

"I pick my friends very carefully. I think one of the more difficult things about being successful is that suddenly everyone wants to be my friend. And that's just not going to work out — at least not for me.

"Without a doubt, every single one of my closest friends has an amazing sense of humor. We pull our senses of humor out of each other when we're together. I don't laugh any harder, ever, than when I'm with . . . well . . . I'm about to name all of my friends!

"I think now, in present times, friendships are put to test an awful lot because people are so mobile. There's a good chance — and this is why I moved Stacey out of Stoneybrook in the Baby-sitters Club for a while — that in almost any group of friends at any age, somebody's going to move away. One proof of friendship is if you can remain close after your friend moves."

6
School Yard Days

Ann started kindergarten at the age of five. As it turned out, there was a hurricane that day, but school wasn't closed. It was only 8:30 in the morning, but the sky had turned as black as night. Ann's mother drove her to school. They got soaked as they ran from the car to the low, squat building of Littlebrook Elementary School. Ann's mother's hat blew off and was lost in the wind.

Inside the building, the lights seemed very bright against the darkness outdoors. Ann didn't like leaving her mother but she liked her first day at school. She especially liked the art projects.

A typical schoolday in the Martin household began with Ann's mom getting the girls washed and ready. She'd have to wake Jane, who liked to sleep late, but Ann usually got up on her own. (Ann has always been an early riser. For a while, her parents made a rule that she couldn't wake them up until after 6:30 in the morning. They made a chart and gave her a star for each day she played quietly. A month's worth of stars would earn her a coloring book or a trip to the movies.) The girls would dress — sometimes in an outfit their mother had handmade for them. Mr. Martin would cook breakfast. Mrs. Martin would pack up lunch in the lunch boxes. Then Ann and Jane would pedal their bikes or walk to school.

It was always a big deal for the girls to pick out their lunch boxes in September, because they were stuck with whatever they chose for the whole year. Ann usually chose a Barbie lunch box, or one decorated with seashells or flowers. Jane picked a Roy Rogers box, or the Munsters.

Littlebrook School was a comfortable place. Ann loved her third-grade teacher, Miss Kushel, who was nice and warmhearted. Miss Kushel didn't yell, and she helped the children accomplish a lot. Ann did very well that year — though she did well most years. She was in the highest reading group. In fact, she was in the highest *everything* group.

Mrs. Dreeben, one of Ann's fourth-grade teachers, was special. She lived on Dodds Lane, nearby the Martins. Mrs. Dreeben says, "Ann was blonde, pretty, very quiet, shy, and very sweet. That's Ann even today, I think. She was such a good child that if there was something she didn't like, she never would have said it. She was a good student, always attentive in all subjects." She adds, "Ann had a lot of thoughts in her mind and

Princeton Township Schools

PRINCETON, NEW JERSEY

REPORT OF PROGRESS

REPORT OF *Ann Martin*

SCHOOL *Littlebrook* GRADE *3*

TEACHER *J. Kushel*

Report to the parents of *Ann Martin* Date *6/44*

READING

Reading book level *Advanced*

	Consistently	Usually	Seldom
He understands what he reads.		✓	
He phrases with comprehension when he reads aloud.	✓		
He identifies words quickly.		✓	
He is able to apply phonics and other word attack skills to figure out new words.	✓		
He remembers word meanings.		✓	
He does the kind of recreational reading necessary to help him develop into a successful reader.	✓		
He reads social studies, science, and reference material with understanding.	✓		

Ann has completed all of the required third grade reading material, supplementary books and an advanced reader.

Ann thinks things out carefully and her comprehension is good. Her reading vocabulary is excellent as is her ability to attack new words phonetically and structurally.

ENGLISH

	Consistently	Usually	Seldom
He can develop an idea orally.			
He can develop an idea in writing.		✓	
He can express his original ideas in writing.		✓	
He spells accurately on spelling tests.			✓
He spells accurately whenever he writes.			
He uses a dictionary to find the correct spelling and the common meaning of words.		✓	
He uses correct grammar in written work.		✓	
He uses correct grammar in conversation.	✓		
He uses capital letters, periods, and question marks correctly.	✓		

Ann continues to write with imagination and she has a good command of the mechanical skills of writing. She is making satisfactory progress in spelling.
Ann takes an active part in classroom discussions.

ARITHMETIC

	Consistently	Usually	Seldom
He can count accurately.	✓		
He can add accurately.	✓		
He can subtract accurately.	✓		
He can multiply accurately. (Grade 3 only)	✓		
He can solve grade level problems.	✓		
He is able to measure time accurately.		✓	
He is able to measure distances and amounts accurately.	✓		

Ann has made an excellent progress in arithmetic this year. She can add, subtract, and write numbers through the millions. She is able to solve one and two step problems. Ann is able to comprehend and think through problems. I hope she will continue to review her multiplication and division facts.

WORK AND STUDY HABITS

	Consistently	Usually	Seldom
He listens to and follows directions.	✓		
He makes good use of time.	✓		
He assumes responsibility for completing work.	✓		
He works neatly and carefully.	✓		
He works independently.	✓		
He puts forth his best effort.	✓		
He makes use of reference materials.	✓		
He writes letter and number forms correctly.		✓	

Ann is a fine, competent worker. She has demonstrated excellent ability.

ATTITUDES

	Consistently	Usually	Seldom
He is courteous to others.	✓		
He respects the rights and opinions of others.	✓		
He exhibits self-control.	✓		
He accepts responsibility.	✓		
He cooperates with the group.	✓		
He requires only a reasonable share of attention.	✓		
He respects school property.	✓		
He abides by the school rules.	✓		

Ann is an outstanding classroom citizen. She is a delightful, happy young lady.
She is to report to Grade 4

Ann's third-grade report card. She already enjoyed writing!

46

all of her work was beautiful, but she was very shy. She hung back and waited for someone else — usually the teacher — to bring her in as part of the group."

Ann liked school. Or rather, she liked the work she had to do at school. The social part was a lot harder for her. She felt uncomfortable being away from her home. She didn't like being with kids she didn't know. If she was feeling bad, or if someone teased her, or if she just wasn't in the mood for the project the class was working on, she just had to put up with it. (I'm sure a lot of you readers know the feeling.)

Ann shined one-on-one. She was never at her best when she was in groups of people. She hated gym class and felt embarrassed to have to do anything in front of the class for any reason. She *still* hates those types of things. She just doesn't have the right kind of personality for them.

Ann says, "School is more than learning and that may have been one reason I didn't like it very much. If school really were just a place to learn to read and write, I would have been fine, but it's a social place, too."

Ann also began to feel the tension of trying to do very, very well. Of course, her parents wanted her to get good grades, but Ann put most of the pressure on herself. She refused to settle for a grade that wasn't top notch. All that pressure made it even harder really to enjoy school. Around this time Ann developed an on-again, off-again nervous stomach, which still troubles her.

Kindergarten

*1st
Grade*

*2nd
Grade*

*3rd
Grade*

*4th
Grade*

*5th
Grade*

School Days — a Collection of School Pictures

*6th
Grade*

*7th
Grade*

*9th
Grade*

*10th
Grade*

*11th
Grade*

Despite her fears and worries, Ann did very well in her classes. In fact, she was mostly an A or high B student (except in math and social studies). Ann's success in school is reflected in some of her teachers' comments on her report cards. Mrs. Love, one of Ann's sixth-grade teachers, wrote, "Ann has made outstanding progress in all areas. She is participating more in class discussions. She has been doing some excellent artwork for the class bulletin boards. I am very pleased with Ann's work this year."

An eighth-grade teacher said, "Ann is a thoughtful and pleasant girl. She understands and applies the fundamental processes well. She must work on her class participation, which isn't on the level that it should be. Her effort and conduct are tops. It is a pleasure to have Ann in class."

And then there's her seventh-grade creative writing teacher's comment: "Excellent! Excellent! Excellent!"

Of course, the social life at school wasn't all bad. For one thing, Ann always had Beth. They'd walk or bike to and from Littlebrook Elementary School together. Later on, they'd ride the schoolbus or take the same car pool. The girls had other friends as well, and together they formed a little group.

Ann and Beth's crowd included Pat Morris, Heidi Faith, and Ruth Gilbert. They might eat lunch together, or meet after school or on weekends. Heidi and Pat were in Ann's sixth-grade class, and the three of them played endless games of jacks. The linoleum classroom floor was perfect for swiping up all the jacks, and it never made the ball bounce crooked.

After school, Ann would head back to Dodds Lane. Her mother, who had gone back to work as a preschool teacher by this time, was always home when her girls returned. Ann would do her homework, practice the piano, or put effort into whatever crafts and projects were in the works at the moment. She might spend a little time at one of her friends' houses.

Ann and her friends adored slumber parties. These might be as small as Ann, Beth, and two of their friends crashing in sleeping bags on someone's bedroom floor, or as big as twenty girls taking over the rec room in Beth's basement. They played games such as Battleship, and other brain teasers. They talked about boys, ate junk food, and maybe made a few goof calls. They also watched movies on TV. There was no such thing as a VCR at the time, so they used to time their slumber parties to when Alfred Hitchcock's classic thriller, *The Birds*, was going to be on.

Though Ann loved the slumber parties, she knew she was best at the small ones — or better yet, one-on-one with friends. She's still like that today.

7
Adventures in Baby-sitting

Ann's first experience with baby-sitting was, of course, when she was a charge herself. Some of her favorite sitters were Johnny McKeever (Beth's older brother), Johnny Valentine, and Nancy Marvel, who lived a few houses down on Dodds Lane. Ann liked Nancy because she treated her as though she were a grown-up. She never talked down to her. The two girls used to have great conversations.

Ann began working as a mother's helper for her neighbors, the Rices, around the age of ten. That was a warm-up for real baby-sitting because Mrs. Rice was around the house. Ann would watch Bo, Carl, and baby Molly while their mother got other chores done. Ann would also help out with the housework.

Ann and Mary B. Rice became good friends.

They'd chat for hours as they cut roses in the gardens or folded the laundry. Ann even tutored Mary B. when she took a French class. (Ann was very good at French herself.)

One summer, the Rices packed up the whole family, including their dog, Pooh (short for Winnie-the-Poodle), and went away to Virginia Beach for a week. Ann came along to be an extra set of eyes on the kids while they played in the water and ran around exploring. Some of those mother's helper scenes at the beach in *Boy-Crazy Stacey, Mary Anne and Too Many Boys,* and *Sea City, Here We Come!* are based on Ann's real experiences.

Ann soon took full responsibility for the Rice kids. She was not a good baby-sitter — she was a fantastic one. She'd bring games and books to the kids (not quite like a Kid-Kit, but pretty close) or think up special art projects and activities.

Mary B. says, "Ann had an intuitive sense about kids. She really listened to them. If Bo or Carl would say something funny, I might just sort of hear it in one ear and do something else at the same time. Ann really heard the humor — which I think is reflected so much in her stories."

A close and special relationship quickly developed between Ann and Molly, the youngest Rice child. Molly loved taking walks and playing outdoors with Ann. And she adored art, just like Ann. One time, Molly drew a picture of a wild-eyed, wild-haired character — the typical kind of thing a three-year-old might color. Ann carefully traced the drawing onto a piece of canvas and needle-pointed it.

Molly loved dressing up, just as Ann had. One year, around Halloween, Ann made her a clown costume — yards of fabric sewn up on a sewing machine — and took her out trick-or-treating. Ann also sewed a pink-and-white dress for Molly's fifth birthday — and she made a copy of the dress in a grown-up size for herself!

Bo and Carl were older than Molly, and didn't need as much supervision from a baby-sitter. Bo, especially, was funny, active, and talkative. Every so often, he'd get into a bit of trouble, and Ann would have to take care of it.

One time, Bo pulled up some jack-in-the-pulpit plants that were growing in the Martins' backyard.

Ann and Molly Rice on Molly's fifth birthday in 1972. Ann made matching outfits as a gift for Molly.

Little did he know that the jack-in-the-pulpits were very, very special to Ann and her sister. So they held a funeral service for the flowers. It made Bo realize that he'd hurt something that was important to someone else.

Carl was kind of accident prone. One time, he got his hand stuck in the vacuum cleaner. Ann calmed him down and helped him get it out. Another time, he caught his foot in the spokes of his bike. It really hurt, and it bled a lot. Ann cleaned up the injured foot as best she could, and waited for Mary B., who was due home shortly. On the lighter side, once the dog across the street ate Carl's socks!

Mary B. says, "A situation would arise, and there was Ann, in the most quiet way possible, without any hoopla or anything, taking care of it." If something *really* bad happened, Ann could always call on her parents for help.

The Rices were good friends with the Martins, so the two families used to spend time together every Christmas. They'd exchange presents and go out for dinner.

Ann's relationship with Molly didn't end when Ann went away to college. It was around this time that Mary B. and Chic Rice got a divorce. Divorce was not as common then as it is now, and the Rices were the first couple Ann knew well who divorced. She realized it must be terribly difficult on Molly, who was seven then, and took a little time out from her studies each week to write to her. She'd go to the school store and buy Molly a gift — just something tiny like a Smith College patch, or a pen with the school's name on it. And Ann continued to baby-sit for Molly when she came home for vacations.

When Ann graduated from college, she invited Molly up for the ceremony. Molly got to sleep in Ann's dorm room and have a special weekend away from home. Later, when Ann moved to New York City, she'd invite Molly over for pizza, or take her to a play. When Mary B. got remarried, Ann offered to take Molly for the night, so the newlyweds could spend their first evening of marriage alone.

Ann baby-sat for other kids, as well as for the Rices. She loved sitting for Wendell Dix, because he was only an infant. Sometimes, Ann would take Wendell to the Rices' to play with Molly. Beth baby-sat for families on the street as well, and often she and Ann would take all the kids out for walks together, or organize a play session.

Beth says, "I admired Ann as being the ultimate baby-sitter. She always had something going on. She showed up with special things to do and ways to entertain the kids. She had this incredible patience about her. She genuinely loved the kids, and they loved her back. There are just some things that you like to do, and you do them well because you're so comfortable with them. Ann was that way with baby-sitting."

Ann continued to baby-sit during her college years. She might drive her charges to the Dairy Queen or to the community pool, which had a snack bar and playground behind it. She'd organize a special day out with the kids. It was as much fun for her as it was for them.

Ann says that all she ever wanted to do when she grew up was to work with kids. They were her passion. That's probably what made her such an amazing baby-sitter.

8
Getting Sick

For the most part, Ann was a healthy child. She got her share of colds and fevers. There were the chicken pox and the mumps, too. And though feeling ill is never any fun, it does have its positive points. For instance, when Ann or Jane was sick, their mother would pull out the Store Bag, which she kept in her closet. Mrs. Martin had filled the bag with coloring books and crayons, toys and art supplies, books and games. The Store Bag was the ancient ancestor of the Kid-Kit.

Ann did have one very serious accident as a child. It happened in the last few weeks of sixth grade, when Ann was eleven years old. She was in the woods in back of her house, playing in the tree house. Mud sculptures were the project of the day. Ann would shape them on the ground, then transport them up to the tree house to dry. Who knows why she thought they had to dry up there, she just did. Beth was helping. Jane was there, too. Jessica Mendlovitz from across the street was playing with the Martins' new bow-and-arrow set.

Earlier in the day, Ann's mother had taken her daughters to Bellow's, a downtown clothing store, to buy new culottes. Culottes are shorts that look like skirts, and they were very popular at the time. Mrs. Martin told the girls not to play in their new clothes outside. Of course, that was the perfect invitation to run right outside in them, so Ann was wearing her new blue-and-white culottes as she made the mud sculptures.

Ann set one batch of sculptures on the wooden floor of the tree house. Then, she started down the old green ladder for some more. She climbed down the ladder frontward, facing away from it, into the woods. One leg of her culottes got hooked on the top of the ladder, and over it went — with Ann on top of it. She fell forward and landed on her front, on top of an old tree stump, the ladder lying on her back. She started screaming. Jessica Mendlovitz thought she'd shot Ann with one of the arrows (she was nowhere near Ann when the accident happened) and went running to get Mrs. Martin.

Ann lay on the ground gasping for breath. The wind had been knocked out of her, but the pain wasn't too bad. Her new culottes were torn, though. In the confusion of the moment, she was most upset about the ruined clothes. She didn't realize yet how seriously she was hurt.

Beth helped Ann up. She seemed okay. Her mother thought maybe she'd bruised her ribs, and decided to call the doctor. Then they drove to Princeton Hospital and the doctors took X rays. He said Ann looked fine, but if her left shoulder began to hurt, they might have to operate. The family stayed at the hospital, and hoped for the best.

Later that night, Ann's left shoulder started to ache. That was bad news. It meant Ann's spleen was damaged and might have to be removed. The spleen is a small organ near the stomach which helps to clean the blood. It's not absolutely necessary, unlike most of the other organs in the body. You can live without one just fine.

The doctors began the operation. In the middle of the night, Chic Rice got a phone call from the hospital saying he was needed to donate blood right away. The next day, it turned out that the blood had been for Ann! Ann was brave. She never even cried.

The operation was a success. Ann stayed in the hospital a week, and healed nicely. She had two roommates who were her own age. The nurse was helpful, concerned, and sweet. Her parents stayed with her as much as they could. Everyone brought presents — flowers, a needlepoint kit, a copy of Louisa May Alcott's classic, *Jo's Boys*, and a new Nancy Drew. Neena and Grandpa happened to be in Princeton on their way up to Maine, and they came to visit Ann often. Being in the hospital meant lots of gifts and attention. And Ann was old enough not to be scared when her parents left.

Ann was *very* dedicated to school. She did all of her homework in the hospital! Her teacher, Mrs. Love, wrote on one assignment, "And to think you were in the hospital!" In fact, that was the one year Ann got straight A's in elementary school — even though she missed the last two weeks of the year.

In those days, children weren't allowed to visit hospital rooms, so neither Jane nor any of Ann's friends could come see her. But the school was only a few blocks from the hospital. During one lunch period, Mrs. Love brought over a group of Ann's friends and classmates. Heidi Faith, Pat Morris, and the other girls stood on the sidewalk outside Ann's second-floor window and called up to her. They had a very nice visit that way.

Ann was beginning to have a beautiful, hour-glass figure around that time, but the operation left a big, vertical scar up her stomach. Ann's father said it looked like a night crawler — one of those extra long worms. Everyone was very proud that Ann continued to wear two-piece bathing suits when they went away to the beach that summer. Many years later, Ann's cousin Margaret had an operation that left a big scar on her own stomach. Aunt Adele held Ann up as a role model and example.

Unfortunately, Ann's encounter with illness does not end here. The result of having her spleen removed is that she gets sick often. She catches colds and flus easily. They take a long time to go away. She also gets tired very easily. This is difficult, especially with a work schedule as heavy as Ann's. Still, Ann says it's a small price to pay for being alive. If she had injured any other organ that badly, she might have died.

In 1981, Ann began showing signs of something which was later diagnosed as an immune system disorder, possibly as a result of having lost her spleen. She often feels as though she has a very, very bad flu for a long, long time. Her joints ache, she runs fevers, and her glands swell. At first, she was tired all day, every day — sometimes too tired even to get out of bed. This first bout of illness lasted six months. At the time, it seemed never ending.

Ann was working as an editor at the Scholastic publishing company at the time. She says, "I missed a lot of days of work at first. There were days when I'd get out of bed in the morning, and maybe I could only make it across the room to an armchair before I'd have to rest again for a little while. Finally, I'd get showered. Sometimes I'd even have to get out of the shower and sit down for a few minutes. Later, I'd make it to the office and put in a short day. Scholastic was very understanding about all of this. Then, slowly, slowly, slowly, I got better."

But the disorder is here to stay. There are still days when Ann feels really lousy. But the bouts never last as long as that first one did.

Ann has found a way to work through her tendency to get sick. She tries to stick to her schedule

Ann on Being Sick

"I know now that there are probably going to be a lot of days when I don't feel well. I've found that the best way to deal with those days is to try to go about them exactly as I had planned, no matter how I feel.

"Of course, if I have a temperature of 102, I'll stay in bed. But if I wake up feeling simply tired and achy — and I do a lot — I find that not only is it better emotionally for me to get up and work, but that I feel better physically, too. It helps me to think of myself as a relatively healthy person instead of a sick one. It helps to exercise and accomplish things rather than giving in to the sick feelings.

"That may not work for everyone who faces illness, but it's the best way for me."

and accomplish as much as she can. She used to stay in bed when she felt tired or ill. But she didn't get better. She just missed work. And lying around all day made her feel like an invalid. She says that when she gets up and concentrates on her writing, she often feels better. Ann also works with a nutritionist to make sure her vegetarian diet is as healthful as possible. She exercises daily and gets a massage once a week, which reduces stress and helps her stay relaxed.

Ann adds, "In terms of reducing stress, I've learned that I don't have to do *every*thing. I don't have to accept every speaking job that comes along — and there are many, many of them. I no longer feel guilty about saying no. If what I happen to need is more time in my apartment by myself relaxing, then that's what I take."

Ann has been healthier in the past few years. Her system must be working.

9
Summer Fun

For many years, summer meant the beach to Ann and her family. Ann first discovered Avalon, on the New Jersey shore, at the age of ten. Beth's family had rented a house there for two weeks, and Ann went on vacation with them. She did that for the next few summers, until her own family began renting a house there.

Avalon was magic. It's a small town that never became very touristy. It sports a miniature golf course, a few simple restaurants, and a small section of boardwalk. Of course, the beach is the main attraction.

Avalon was so tiny and safe that Ann and Beth could always go out on their own. In the morning, they'd ride their bikes to Hoy's, where they could get an entire breakfast for sixty-nine cents. They'd eat at the counter. After that, they'd ditch their

*Hanging out on a lifeguard's chair in Avalon. That's
Beth, Ann, Jane, and Ann's father.*

bikes at the house and walk the few blocks to the
beach. They'd swim, make drip castles in the sand,
sunbathe, take walks along the water, or go to the
jetty to watch people fish.

Later in the afternoon, they might head back into
town and windowshop, or buy fried food at Kwik-
Kook to eat on the beach. It was great to be so
independent.

It was almost impossible to get bored in Avalon.
But if for some strange reason you did, there was
always Wildwood, which is just a couple of towns
away. Wildwood has everything — especially an
elaborate boardwalk with rides, games, and dozens
of fast food places and souvenir shops. Purple plastic palm trees line the streets. This was where the

teenagers went on dates, and where Ann went, too, when she got a bit older.

Baby-sitters Club fans may be wondering why Avalon and Wildwood sound so familiar. It's because Ann used those towns and another, Surf City, as a model for Sea City, where Mallory's family goes for their summer vacations. She combined aspects of all three towns.

If you've read *Boy-Crazy Stacey*, you'll recognize the next story, which was the basis for that book. When Ann and Beth were about twelve, they began to notice the lifeguards. So did a lot of other girls on the beach. Ann and Beth would play in the waves directly in front of the lifeguard chairs, or hang around with the rest of the love-struck girls, hoping they'd be singled out of the bunch.

Summer days in Avalon.
Ann at fourteen in 1969.

One time, they were. A cute lifeguard asked Ann and Beth to bring him lunch. The girls were thrilled. They ran back to Beth's house. Unfortunately, it was one of those days when there was absolutely nothing exciting in the kitchen. They made a few peanut butter-and-jelly sandwiches, but they didn't have any plastic bags, so they just put them back in the bag the bread had come in. Then they grabbed a few sodas and headed back to the beach.

Of course, there was no chance that any of the lifeguards were going to ask Ann or Beth on a date. They were much older. But they would talk and flirt. If they hadn't, how would they have gotten their free lunches?

Since Ann's birthday is in August, it often fell during one of the vacations in Avalon. On that day, Ann would usually ride her bike over to Beth's house early — and I mean *very* early. Beth would crawl out her window, they'd hop on their bikes, and they'd ride to the doughnut shop. They'd buy as many doughnuts as they could carry while riding their bikes, and go down to the jetty at the beach. They'd sit there, eating doughnuts and talking. Then they'd ride home and get there in time for breakfast.

The Martins often had visitors at Avalon. Neighbors from Dodds Lane came. So did Aunt Adele, Uncle Paul, and their kids. Aunt Adele reports that they had one absolutely glorious visit, partly because Ann was wonderful with Margaret, who was only two or three at the time. She says, "Ann's love of children and her total adeptness with them was incredible." Ann would tell Margaret about Molly Rice, and Margaret would eat up the stories.

Aunt Adele and her family returned to Avalon in 1971, just after Grandpoppy had died. This time, they brought Granny with them. Everyone was trying to cheer Granny up. They played the card game Hearts every night, and tried to laugh a lot. Aunt Adele says that Ann, especially, was very sensitive to how Granny was feeling.

The Martin parents used to plan one big trip for the summer. Often it was to Avalon, but sometimes they'd drive to Maine and visit with Neena and Grandpa. Those trips included hiking and lobster eating. The family would also go to the sardine canning factory nearby and watch the workers' hands flying over their tasks. Ann could never believe how fast they were.

Twice the Martins traveled west. When Ann was thirteen, they flew to Denver, then caught a sleeper train to San Francisco, California. The train had a big glass dome on the top, so the passengers could look out and see everything. The train trip took two whole days. Ann had read *Harriet the Spy*, by Louise Fitzhugh. She and Jane spent the entire time spying on people and writing notes about them in their secret notebook.

The family spent a few days seeing the sites in San Francisco. Then they rented a car, packed it to the top with all their stuff, and visited Disneyland and several national parks. They went horseback riding in the mountains and swam in quiet lakes. They drove their car through a tunnel made in the center of a huge redwood tree. They saw Old Faithful in Yellowstone Park.

During another trip, they flew to California, then drove east to Milwaukee, Wisconsin, where Mrs. Martin had grown up. They stopped at the house she had lived in as a child. They saw Lake Oconomowoc, where she had spent her own summer vacations when she was small. Ann enjoyed the peek into her mother's childhood. They also saw Flintstone Park. Jane, especially, was dying to visit this fake Bedrock. Unfortunately Fred wasn't there the day the Martins were, having been stoned by a visitor the day before.

Ann did a lot of reading in the car. Sometimes, her father got annoyed. He'd have planned the trip practically down to the minute, and Ann would be passing everything by with her nose inside a novel. Jane got carsick if she read, so she got out a pack of cards for endless rounds of solitaire.

The family played a lot of car games. They'd try to spot license plates from every state. Mrs. Martin taught the girls to sing rounds and each family member took a part. They sang "Old Bill Bailey," "Dona Nobis Pacem," and "Tender Shepherd" from the Broadway show *Peter Pan*. Mrs. Martin also brought along games and toys from the Store Bag.

At least once during each trip, Ann and Jane would end up in a big fight. (Don't all sisters and brothers fight on long car trips?) Their parents would divide up the backseat so that each girl could have her own space. Of course, that often gave them one more reason to fight. Cries of "She went over the line" and "Don't touch me! Don't touch me!" rang through the car.

Sometimes the girls would fight with their parents, too. Usually, those arguments started when the girls got a little too silly. They'd say, "How many more minutes until we get there?" practically a million times. And then, when they knew they were really bugging their parents, they'd ask again.

Ann wrote letters and postcards home to Beth and her other friends. She usually picked up souvenirs for her friends — the tackier the better. She'd buy a big plastic back scratcher or a silly hat. Beth still has a china deer Ann bought for her at Yellowstone National Park. Ann can't resist a funny gift at a souvenir shop. A few years ago, she went to Las Vegas for ABA (that's a conference of writers, publishers, booksellers, and just about anyone else who has anything to do with books). She brought back a plastic show girl doll. The doll's costume is so tight, it's actually painted on.

During the summer weeks when the family wasn't on a trip or at the beach, Ann baby-sat, worked on art projects, and needlepointed. And she read, read, read. She never had any trouble keeping herself busy. She'd also go swimming with Beth and her other friends, attend slumber parties, and generally hang around. She loved just relaxing and unwinding after the pressure of school.

Ann never went to sleep-away camp. She didn't

like the idea of being away from her parents. She didn't want to be someplace where she didn't know the other kids. And she was always a picky eater. You know all those books Ann wrote about summer camp? She made them up from things her friends *told* her about camp!

The Martins didn't go to Europe when the children were young, but they made up for it later. When Jane was spending part of her junior year in college studying in England and Ann was already out of college and working, she and her parents flew to London to meet Jane and drive around the English countryside. The high point of the trip was visiting Hilltop, where the great children's book writer Beatrix Potter, (the author of *Peter Rabbit*) had once lived. The family returned to Europe three years later. Ann spent a weekend in Paris that time. She *loved* it. She wants to go back there more than any place in the world.

As an adult, Ann spent a few marvelous summers at a beach very different from Avalon. She and some of her friends rented a house on Fire Island. There were about eight of them in all. That was when Ann and her friend Michelle Rapkin had a chance to become close.

The town of Davis Park on Fire Island is about two and a half hours from New York City. No cars are allowed on the island, and it can be reached only by ferry. There are no sidewalks, just narrow wooden walkways between the houses. Davis Park consists of one big restaurant-disco, which Ann mainly avoided, and a small general store.

Ann and her friends were working very hard in New York, and at the end of the week, they'd all be ready to relax. They'd have long heart-to-heart talks as the train chugged out of the city. Then they'd board the ferry to Fire Island, breathing in the salt air and feeling the excitement of the coming weekend.

Silliness was the mood of the house. They bought a Mr. Potato Head. They held a silly contest that lasted the entire summer. The prize was a tacky crocheted vest, which no one would ever have dared to wear. A few people — including Ann — had summer birthdays. They'd celebrate by decorating the house with crepe paper swirls and balloons, and getting gallons and gallons of ice cream.

Usually, though, the weekend was quiet. The friends would spend the days sitting on the beach, devouring books, taking walks and swimming. Ann, in particular, read a lot. She went through many novels, several biographies, a few Stephen King stories, and a number of children's books.

Ann and her friends used to watch the sunset from a nearby wildlife preserve. If they were lucky, they'd spot deer or rabbits. Or they'd sit out on the deck with a cold drink and watch the sun sink behind the roofs of the other houses.

They always made a Saturday night dinner. Usually, they cooked something simple, like barbecued hot dogs and hamburgers or fresh fish. After dinner, they'd play Trivial Pursuit or cards, and tell funny family stories. They also made miniature wax sculptures from candle drippings. The best of these were preserved in the freezer, and they had an exhibit at the end of the summer.

Ice cream pig-outs were popular. Michelle says it was especially fun to watch Ann — who doesn't usually eat a whole lot of *anything* — go wild. A favorite flavor was Heath Bar Crunch, but usually several different flavors were stored in the freezer at any one time. Peanut M&M's were also an important house treat.

It was always a fun weekend. By the time Ann and her friends started back for the city on Sunday, they were exhausted from playing so hard. They'd sleep or read on the train home.

The first year Ann took the house with Michelle, she was just beginning to write the Baby-sitters Club books. The other people in the house would go back to New York to jobs in publishing, banking, or law, and Ann would go back to her apartment to work on *The Truth About Stacey*.

Later, Ann wrote two books set on Fire Island. One is called *Eleven Kids, One Summer*. The other is called *Just a Summer Romance*. If you read this one, you'll notice a lot of things slipping through from Ann's real life — peanut M&M's and ice cream bashes, for instance. Melanie Braderman shares some characteristics with Ann. For example, she enjoys being alone, hates being the new kid, likes school but is nervous about it, and is imaginative, creative, and funny. But they are definitely not the same person. Actually, this is a pretty common writing technique. An author takes details from his or her own life, and transforms them into something similar but not quite the same.

Unfortunately, the romance part of *Just a Summer Romance* is fictional. Ann didn't meet any gorgeous TV stars on Fire Island. But she and her friends had a great time together, just enjoying each other's company.

Ann and her friends shared beach houses for several more summers. Just before the last one, though, the doctor told Ann that she had to stay out of the sun, which was dangerous for her skin. That year, she went to the beach wearing long sleeved shirts and light pants, with her David Letterman baseball cap — sort of like Mary Anne in the Baby-sitters Club. After that, she decided to avoid beaching.

Now Ann's vacations include visiting friends in other towns or relaxing at home. She likes having a few weeks off in New York City. She can relax, catch up on sewing projects, go to the theater, and spend time with friends. She also goes to her country house near the mountains where the trees provide a lot of shade. That way, Ann can get out of the city and relax, but stay out of the sun at the same time.

10
Events and Family Outings

The serious business of eating hot dogs at Ann's sixth birthday party. Beth is on the far left, and Jane is peeking out from behind her.

Birthdays were always important events around the Martins' house. Mr. and Mrs. Martin planned special parties, with lots of friends, entertainment, and a home-baked birthday cake. Sometimes the entertainment was something simple. Once, when the girls were very young, the party guests took a ride on the Dinky. That's the two-car train that travels between the tiny station in Princeton to the main station in Princeton Junction. The trip takes only five minutes, and would be pretty boring for an older child. But for the little kids, it was like riding on their own private train. At another birthday, everyone went on a pony ride.

When Ann turned eight, her parents hired a magician to perform at her party. He let Ann help with the tricks. That was thrilling, because she was beginning to be interested in performing magic herself at the time. Her father had interested her in it. He used to put on amateur magic shows. When Ann showed an interest, he gave her all his old tricks. Later, when Ann went on to other hobbies, they gave the tricks to a younger kid who wanted to learn them.

The entire Martin family loves Broadway musical shows. They used to go to New York City often to have lunch and see a matinee. Jane says, "When we went into the tunnel beneath the Hudson River, Dad said, 'Now when we come out of the tunnel, we'll be in New York City.' And at first we were bummed out because it was not too much different than New Jersey. We thought that it would be like Oz or something, this gleaming, beautiful city. And it was just streets and buildings."

For lunch, the family would usually go to Schrafft's, which is known for its enormous ice cream sundaes. Two of their favorite shows were *Annie Get Your Gun* and *Hello, Dolly!*

Circuses were also important to the Martins, especially Ann's father. Each year, the Hunt Brothers' small three-ring circus would come to Princeton. Mr. Martin would wake up his daughters early (actually, Ann would already have woken up on her own), and they'd watch the roustabouts raising the big-top tent. It took a few hours for the crew to set up the circus. After that, the Martins would go home for lunch, and return later for the show. There was also a yearly pilgrimage into the city when the Ringling Brothers' Circus came to town. Ann still sees many of the different circuses that pass through New York.

Ann loved all the acts except the clowns. She was afraid of the masklike makeup. She especially hated it when they'd try to play with her. She was never quite sure how to react.

The Martins never missed the Princeton University reunions. All of Ann's father's buddies from college — and hundreds of other Princeton students, Princeton graduates, and their families — descend on the town one weekend in June. They hold class meals, parties with dance bands, and picnics.

And there's the P-rade (short for the Princeton Parade). Each class of Princeton graduates marches together, sometimes with their families. Every group carries signs and has a class costume. The costume might be black-and-orange shorts or a special kind of hat. Ann and Jane marched with their father's class. They sometimes wore a variation on the costume, which their mother had sewn especially for the P-rade.

There were other activities that the family enjoyed together — or that the girls *made* their parents do. For instance, Ann and Jane were pretty excited about questionnaires for a while. One time, Ann made one for her parents. It was *long* and it covered *everything*. One question was, "Loves her children?" Ann's mother, of course, answered, "YES!"

Ann liked to make up imaginary menus for dinners. Sometimes, around the time of a special event or a birthday, her mother would actually make the meal.

Another important event for Ann and Jane was going to the Estys' house to watch *The Wizard of Oz* on their big, color TV. The Estys were good friends with Ann's parents. Val Esty was like Ann's third grandmother. Watching *The Wizard of Oz* on their color TV was special because the beginning scenes of the movie are in black-and-white, but when Dorothy lands in Oz, everything turns to color. That moment when she opens the door of her little black-and-white house and sees the Technicolor flowers of Oz should not be missed.

One morning, after an airing of *The Wizard of Oz* the night before, Ann and Jane came downstairs to find that their father had set out all the supplies they'd need to make papier mâché puppets of the characters in the movie. Together, they created Dorothy, the Tin Woodsman, the Lion, the Scarecrow, and the Wicked Witch of the West. Their mother helped them sew clothes for the puppets.

The Martins had their own private tradition for welcoming autumn. The family would make vegetable soup over an outdoor fire in the woods behind the house. Dad would set up stones or bricks in a circle. The girls would find firewood. Mom would bring out a pot and a soup bone. The family would sit around cutting up the veggies and waiting for the water to boil. When the soup was done, they'd eat it outside.

Ann's parents made sure their daughters had fun and active childhoods. Perhaps that is why family is so important to Ann today.

Jane and Ann with their father. Their mother captured them cooking vegetable soup in the woods behind their house.

11
High School

Princeton High School is a beautiful stone building with a tower. It looks more like a college than a typical high school. Behind the school are the tennis courts and the football field. It is an excellent school, and once was one of the top ten public high schools in America. Unfortunately, it was also very crowded when Ann attended it. Some classes took place in other buildings nearby (which the kids called outhouses).

The main focus for Ann in high school was *work*! It was incredibly important to her to keep her grades up, and she sacrificed a lot of social time to do it. She took five courses, instead of the usual four, in ninth, tenth and eleventh grades.

Ann's favorite classes were always English and French. It isn't surprising Ann is a writer now. She works all day long with words. So of course she enjoyed and did well in the classes that had to do with language.

Art classes were also a joy for Ann. She adored drawing, painting, crafts, anything. It was nice that the art teachers didn't come down too hard on the students — though there were some pretty tough assignments.

The school had many experimental programs that made learning fun and interactive (not just reading textbooks). Ann liked those classes best.

Even though Ann was an excellent student, there were, of course, a few subjects she just hated. Math, for example. She was always in the second to lowest math class, and usually earned B's. Ann just never understood mathematical ideas very well. In fact, she is still bad at math. She uses calculators — or counts on her fingers when a calculator isn't handy.

History was also not a favorite subject of Ann's. She had to work extremely hard at it, but she usually managed to do well in the end.

Despite her problems with math, Ann was on the honor role every year of high school. She took so many classes each year that she could have graduated halfway through her senior year. Ann also did a lot of volunteer work and baby-sitting during high school. She was very busy.

One result of working so hard for the first three years of high school was that Ann's senior year was a lot less pressured. She took child care, horticulture, home ec, English, and French — some of her favorite classes. Ann felt guilty about having such an easy year after working so hard for the first three. She had always pushed herself, and it was hard to put the work behind her — even though she deserved it.

The child care class turned out to be a very special experience for Ann. The students in the class were preparing to start a preschool. Ann had always wanted to become a teacher, so this was a golden opportunity for her. The class spent the first half of the year planning the preschool, and the second half running it. Three- and four-year-old kids attended it for an hour and a half each day. It was for children who needed an early schooling experience, but weren't ready to be away from their parents for very long. Of course, Ann *loved* it.

Ann also adored her horticulture class. Mr. Toscano (better known as Mr. T.) was a memorable teacher. He was probably the best teacher Ann ever had for anything. He made the subject come alive, and most of the students loved the class so much that they actually enjoyed doing the homework.

As always, Beth was an important part of Ann's social life when she was in high school. Ann, Beth, Nancy Jacobs, Karen Loar, and a few other girls would eat the horrible cafeteria food together and talk about choir, sports, and upcoming dances.

The girls were a studious group and they always followed the school rules. The high school was near the downtown area of Princeton, and many kids sneaked out to the pizzeria or nearby hamburger joints. Ann and her friends never did, even though they could have gotten a much better lunch.

Beth and the other girls in Ann's circle belonged to the choir. Being in the singing group was a real honor. The Princeton High choir was very good. They traveled to Europe one summer, and gave concerts around the Princeton area as well.

Ann never tried out for the choir — not because she had a bad voice, but because she just couldn't stand the idea of auditioning. She would have had to stand up in front of Mr. Trego, the choir director, and *all the other kids who were trying out*, and sing by herself. Ann was sure she would have done fine during actual performances. Eighty other voices would have been singing along with hers. But to sing totally on her own? Uh-uh, there was no way.

Ann didn't feel left out, though. She came to choir practices at times when she had a free period and just listened. She helped raise money for choir trips through bake sales. She was always excited for her friends when they performed. She felt lonely, however, when they went off to Europe one summer and Ann was left behind in Princeton.

Social events included shopping in the stores on Nassau Street, going to the movies and school dances, and having more slumber parties. In addition, several of Ann's friends were candy stripers at the hospital along with her. These and other volunteer activities, such as working in the Red Cross Youth Group, were some of Ann's after-school activities.

Ann at sixteen. Miniskirts were in!

Ann and Beth both had friends outside their little group — though not necessarily the same ones. If one of them began spending more time with somebody else, they knew they could come back to each other at any time. Theirs was a solid friendship.

School wasn't always fun. Ann loved reading, but she wanted to pick her own books, not have to spend most of her time on the ones her teachers assigned. She loved studying, but not the tension of worrying about grades and tests. She explains, "I was very good in school but it was always a struggle. I felt I didn't understand things — or didn't understand them fast enough. But after all that nervousness, every marking period I'd end up with great grades and good test scores." The anxiety made school a lot less comfortable than it could have been.

The social aspect of school could also be difficult for Ann. She loved her friends, but couldn't avoid some of the snobbier kids who made fun of anyone who wasn't part of their group. Ann says, "There is a bunch of snobby kids at every high school. At Princeton High some of them picked on me and some of them picked on other kids. And probably, they were picked on by other kids themselves."

Ann particularly hated study halls. They were held in the cafeteria, so there were literally hundreds of kids sitting together, supposedly working. Of course, no one did. It was too noisy to study even if you wanted to. Ann hated the idea of sitting there, wasting all that time. When she was lucky, she could sign up to go to the library for study hall.

One of the worst things that happened to Ann in high school was when another kid stole her horticulture paper out of her locker. She had spent weeks and weeks on the paper. The other student didn't use it as her own — she just didn't want Ann to hand in something that good. She was jealous of how well Ann was doing in the class. Ann didn't tell on the other girl because she was afraid to cause trouble.

Everything worked out okay in the end. Mr. Toscano believed Ann when she said her work had been stolen — he knew she was an honest kid who wasn't just making up an excuse. Then Ann asked Mr. T. if she could hand in a makeup project. She created a herbarium — a detailed display of leaves from all the plants in the area. She identified each plant and included important information about it. It was even *better* than the first project.

Ann did go to football and basketball games, but really only because her friends were going. She wasn't all that interested in the games themselves. But she liked being with the girls. They'd bring along boyfriends, too, whenever one of them happened to be seeing someone special.

Ann went to the senior prom with a sweet guy named Lowell Johnson. She bought a long, floor-length dress made out of orange-and-yellow flower print fabric, and wrapped a white shawl around her shoulders. At the time, she thought she looked beautiful, but looking back at the pictures today, she can only laugh. The prom was held at the Nassau Inn, a lovely hotel in downtown Princeton with a big dance room. All of Ann's friends were there with their boyfriends or dates — Beth, Nancy, Karen, and the others. Everyone had a great time.

But not Ann. She felt shy. She spent a lot of time hanging back, trying *not* to dance. Though many of the kids went out after the prom for a beach party, Ann skipped it. Parties and dances simply have never been for her.

Ann graduated from high school in 1973 with high honors. All that hard work paid off.

12
Christmas Spirit

Anyone who knows Ann is aware of how important Christmas is to her. She goes all out, with presents for everyone she knows, a party, donations to needy people, and lots of holiday decorations. The holiday has always been very special to her.

Ann's family felt that the best way to celebrate Christmas was with family and friends. A few times, the Martins went to Louisville to spend the holidays with the Kentucky relatives — Granny and Grandpoppy, Aunt Adele and her family, and Uncle Lyman and his wife and children. The Martins used to dress up for Christmas Day back then. There are pictures of Ann wearing velvet dresses with lace collars. Now they're more casual about what they wear.

The weeks before December 25th were always

Ann at three, celebrating Christmas at her grandparents'
house in Louisville. She's very intent on opening
that gift.

busy. The family would make tree decorations and
cookies. The girls' father would take them shopping for their mother and Mom would take them
shopping for Dad. Ann enjoyed wrapping the
presents and decorating the house.

Mr. Martin taught his daughters a special way
to send letters to Santa. They would slip their toy
requests over the fire roaring in the fireplace. The
current created by the hot air would suck the letter
up the chimney and, Mr. Martin said, into Santa's
box at the North Pole.

On Christmas Eve, the kids would hang empty
stockings from the fireplace mantelpiece. They'd
put out cookies and a note for Santa. In the morning, the gifts their parents said Santa had brought
would be in front of the now stuffed stockings.

The presents the adults *admitted* they bought for the children would be under the tree.

On Christmas morning, the kids would get started early — as early as they could get away with. They weren't allowed to wake their parents until at least five in the morning. Everyone would be downstairs by 5:05. Within fifteen minutes, the presents would be opened, wrapping paper and ribbons would be everywhere, and the girls would be engrossed in games.

The big secret about Ann and Christmas is that she never believed in Santa Claus. Not even when she was a tiny little kid. She liked the *idea* of Santa, but when she looked around at all her presents — some of which were pretty large — she realized that no one could ever bring that much stuff to every child in the world. Ann had a practical mind, even then.

As Ann became a little older, she and Beth began a Christmas tradition that lasts to this day. They would spend the day before Christmas together, probably to help pass the time when they absolutely could not wait another second for the big day to come. They'd sing carols, make a Christmas mural, and exchange presents.

Ann's family would have Christmas Eve dinner with the Rices. Often, they'd eat at Good Time Charlie's. It wasn't a fancy restaurant, but it had a nice, family feeling to it. It was a place where people could enjoy themselves during the holiday season.

The Martins often spent Christmas Day with Uncle Rick and Aunt Merlena's family or with the Valentines. Christmas Day dinner might be turkey or roast beef, with vegetables and potatoes. Or Mrs. Martin would set out a buffet. Everyone could make a sandwich with all the things he or she liked best. They'd sit in front of the fire, eating and talking.

Aunt Adele reports that Ann always made presents and decorations for Christmas and sent them down to Kentucky. She sewed pincushions and made other small gifts. She created beautiful Christmas tree ornaments, too. One of Aunt Adele's favorites was a pink sphere with pearls. Aunt Adele has saved all Ann's homemade ornaments, and she still uses them to decorate her family's tree.

Ann says, "Christmas has become so important to our family because of the traditions. It's also a time of togetherness, friendship, and fellowship. And now that Jane and I are grown up, it's the one day of the year my family knows for sure all four of us are going to be together!" Ann always returns home for Christmas. That way, she gets to see her family, Uncle Rick and Aunt Merlena, the Rices, and Beth and her family as well.

Just as Ann used to spend Christmas Eve day with Beth, she now spends it with Beth's family. Ann and the Perkinses like to try a special activity, like creating gingerbread houses. Beth buys boxes of graham crackers, bags of peppermints and M&M's, and jars of icing. Everyone builds and decorates her own. Once, Gabbie decided to turn her house into a space station. (She filled it completely with M&M's before putting the roof on and icing it, so she could snack on them when the holidays were over.) Gabbie stuck long, flat strands of licorice around the outside of the house. They looked like monorail tracks. Ann shot pictures that day, but she forgot to put film in her camera. Luckily, Beth's photos came out fine. Gabbie reports that the space station tasted great!

Christmas wouldn't be complete without gifts. One of Ann's Christmas gifts to the Perkins girls was a set of tickets to see *Les Misérables*, the Broadway show. She also likes to buy them toys, clothes and, of course, books.

Ann spends incredible amounts of time preparing for Christmas. She goes shopping six, eight, even eleven months in advance. Yes, Ann actually begins preparing for Christmas just as soon as she has recovered from the bustle of the last one! All year long, she shops at toy stores or in catalogs. The gift then goes into her Christmas closet, which is a legend among her friends. When the right time comes, she'll go into the closet and pick out exactly the right gift. She makes sure her presents are beautifully wrapped, with lots of ribbons and tinsel. They are really fun to open.

Ann likes to give toy gifts or joke gifts to some of her adult friends. One of her favorites was a mirror that laughed at you when you picked it up. She ordered fourteen of them. Baby-sitters Club fans may remember this toy from *Stacey's Emergency*. Ann also likes to give books and flowers.

One of Ann's recent Christmas cards. The message inside read:
Hoping your holidays are warm and cozy — greetings from Ann and Mouse and Rosie!

Ann's newest Christmas tradition is her yearly party. She hires a caterer, has the apartment cleaned from top to bottom, pulls out her favorite Christmas decorations, and invites everyone she knows. The house smells like hot cider and pine needles.

The party usually takes place on a Saturday afternoon a week or two before Christmas. Her friends arrive dressed in holiday clothes. They bring their children, many of whom are wearing outfits Ann handmade for them. There is a gift under the tree for every child who comes to the party. Ann also puts out art supplies, and the kids make decorations and drawings.

Ann has given away many Christmas toys to kids in homeless shelters. Every December she goes to Kiddie City and fills up three shopping carts with games, dolls, stuffed animals, balls, and everything else you can imagine. Actually, it's as much fun for Ann as it is for the kids. She loves buying toys.

For Ann, it really is as much fun to give as to receive at Christmastime. In fact, it's the tradition and the sharing that she enjoys most, not getting presents. During the Christmas season, Ann reaches out to everyone she likes and cares about. She feels the warmth and support of her family and friends drawing close.

13
Tastes

Ann may be shy and quiet, but she knows what she likes and what she doesn't. And she'll tell you, if you ask her. Ann's style isn't fancy, but she likes things of good quality. She has simple, traditional, classic taste.

Ann has a neat but casual way of dressing. You can usually find her in jeans, a polo shirt or sweat shirt, and white sneakers. She likes to be comfortable. She's not trendy at all, and doesn't follow fashion fads. She loves sweaters and earrings, and has a big collection of both. Her earrings run from a classic pair of pearls to a pair that's a jingly mishmash of plastic toys, including miniature cowboy boots!

When Ann gets dressed up, she wears dresses and jumpers made of tasteful flower-printed material. They are simple, but well cut. Every so often,

*Ann in 1992,
happily wearing
one of her
usual casual outfits.*

you'll see her in a dress with a lace collar. She *never* wears high heels.

Ann swears she doesn't look good without makeup. Her friends ask, "What makeup?" Usually, it's just a little cover stick to smooth out her pale, clear complexion, plus a hint of mascara and rouge. If she's really getting decked out, she might use a tiny bit of eyeliner. She hates lipstick and only wears it for photo shoots. Then she wipes it off. She thinks it's uncomfortable and smells funny.

Today, Ann considers herself a vegetarian (she does enjoy fish, too) and has a very healthful diet. But her diet isn't about losing weight. In fact, there have been times when Ann has made a real effort to *gain* weight. Her diet was designed to help her stay as strong and healthy as possible. Ann is a vegetarian because she doesn't like meat, but also because she thinks it isn't very good for you.

There are a lot of things Ann doesn't like to eat, such as shellfish, cabbage, and anything with mayonnaise in it. There are also a lot of things she adores but tries to avoid because they aren't healthy, such as ice cream and chocolate. She does have a sweet tooth, but she doesn't indulge herself much. Actually, she doesn't have trouble staying away from the sweets. The trick is not keeping them in the house in the first place, because if they're there, she'll be tempted to eat half the package.

When Ann was a child, her mother was the household cook. She made dishes such as meat loaf or chicken, with vegetables on the side. The Martin family rule was that you didn't have to clean your plate, but you did have to taste at least a forkful of everything. This got dicey when squash was served. (Ann likes squash now, however.)

Dad was the breakfast cook. He was very attentive about the food. During the phase when Jane refused to eat anything but poached egg yolks, he'd dutifully strain away the whites without a complaint. One time, though, he created an entirely new breakfast dish completely by accident. He dubbed the dish "Stuck Door Eggs." Jane tells the story of them:

"One time, Dad was making scrambled eggs. He tried to open the front door to get the paper, and the door was stuck. He hassled with it and jimmied around with it, and, finally, it opened. But by the time he got back to the stove, the eggs were hard. They weren't bad. They were kind of like an omelette. Of course, he didn't want to start over again, and we were old enough so that we should have been able to deal with it. So he played it up, saying that he'd made this great new dish called Stuck Door Eggs. And we *loved* it. And now, we never have scrambled eggs in our house, we always have Stuck Door Eggs." And Jane jokes, "Stuck Door Eggs should definitely make it into Ann's biography, because it could become a new taste treat for the United States."

The lunches Ann and Jane brought to school usually included a peanut butter-and-jelly or bologna sandwich wrapped in wax paper, with a piece of fruit, or cut carrots. For a while, Mom banned Twinkies. Ann and Jane had to have a mini-revolt so they could get them back. Finally, their mother said okay, but they had to eat the Twinkies only *after* they finished their fruit.

Ann doesn't have a lot of time for hobbies, but she *makes* time for her sewing, needlework, and smocking. She developed her lifelong love of these hobbies very early on. They are crafts her mother and grandmothers have enjoyed. When Ann was a sophomore in high school, she spent months and months saving up to buy a sewing machine of her own. Then she began to make a lot of her own clothes. She kept it up until college, when she just didn't have the time anymore.

Today, Ann sews and smocks a great deal, but

says that it's too hard to take her own measurements and fit things for herself. All of her current sewing projects are outfits for her friends' children. Recently, she made a baby sunsuit with cacti and cowboys smocked across the top and buttons shaped like little cowboy hats. Another project was a blue flowered dress with a white pinafore over it and smocking showing some teddy bears having a picnic.

Ann is beginning to be a collector of beautiful glass. She has bought a few very special paperweights and perfume bottles. She also collects the children's books that have won the Newbery and Caldecott awards. These include *A Wrinkle in Time* by Madeleine L'Engle and *The Polar Express* by Chris Van Allsburg.

As you may have guessed already, Ann was and is a *big* reader. As a child, her nose was always buried in a book. Now, she doesn't have as much time to read, so she treasures the time she spends reading before bed. On vacations, she slowly whittles away at her very long book list. She says, "Books are a pathway to all kinds of worlds. Even if you're stuck in bed, you can read about other countries, even other planets."

As a child, Ann read many classic children's books such as Frances Hodgson Burnett's *The Secret Garden*, L. Frank Baum's Wizard of Oz series, Lewis Carroll's *Alice in Wonderland* and Hugh Lofting's *Doctor Dolittle*. She also enjoyed the more modern books of Roald Dahl, the Marguerite Henry horse stories, Astrid Lindgren's Pippi

Longstocking books, Richard and Florence Atwater's *Mr. Popper's Penguins,* and Betty MacDonald's Mrs. Piggle Wiggle books. She read a lot of fantasy and imaginative stories. She liked reading about things that could never happen in real life, and trips to far and distant imaginary lands.

In high school and college, she read a lot of science fiction, particularly the books of Ray Bradbury and Isaac Asimov. She has also always enjoyed funny books.

Now, Ann likes realistic books most. Some of her favorite adult writers are Jamaica Kincaid, E. L. Doctorow, Lynn Sharon Schwartz, and Chaim Potok. They write stories about things that could really happen. It's not surprising, then, to learn that Ann reads a lot of nonfiction, too. She especially likes biographies of authors and books with a psychological basis.

Ann was also a big mystery novel reader. She started out with Nancy Drew and the Bobbsey Twins, which were books her mother had loved as a child. Years later, when Ann worked in the field of publishing, she edited some of the new Nancy Drew and Bobbsey Twins stories. Ann was a good reader, and she soon graduated to the adult mysteries of Agatha Christie. As a teenager, Ann always brought one or two Christie mysteries to Avalon in the summer. They were perfect for curling up with on those rare rainy days.

Ann likes to try to figure out the endings to the mysteries she reads. She says, "I'm very bad. If I think I've figured out the solution or if the solution is driving me crazy, I *will* peek at the last page before I've read the rest of the book." But she always goes back and finishes the novel because she likes to see how the author handled the story. It helps her learn how to write her own stories and mysteries.

The Martin girls watched a fair amount of TV. The day often started out with *Captain Kangaroo* before school. In later years, the family would gather around the TV set and howl over *The Addams Family* and *Get Smart*. And of course, there was Lucy. Ann loves every episode. She's even memorized a couple of sections, most notably, the Vitameatavegamin commercial. (Lucy fans will know what that means.) She owns almost the entire series of *I Love Lucy* shows on videotape.

Today, Ann watches *Seinfeld, Cheers, Designing Women, Roseanne, Saturday Night Live,* and *David Letterman* — though Letterman is on too late for her to catch it often. All of these are shows that make her laugh out loud. She pays attention to the way funny scenes are written, because she writes a lot of funny scenes in her own books. Ann also watches *Full House* and *The Wonder Years* because she knows they're favorites with many of the kids who read her books.

Ann doesn't watch much TV, though, anymore. In fact, there aren't any shows she'll actually take the trouble to tape on her VCR if she can't watch them when they're aired. She says, "I try to limit the amount of television that I watch because it can be a real waste of time."

Ann Talks About TV and Violence

"I think an awful lot of cartoons are much too violent. Kids learn — wrongly — that violence doesn't really hurt other people because they see a cartoon character get bopped over the head forty times, and then he's fine. As a parent, you have to be careful of what your children watch. There are some fine cartoons, and there are some I don't think anyone should watch.

"It's the same with other kinds of TV shows. For instance, *The Cosby Show* presents a very nice family with wonderful values. They make mistakes, just like real families do, but they love each other very much. That's what comes through in the end. And that's a lovely thing to learn.

"If kids park themselves in front of the TV and watch *The Cosby Show* for thirty minutes, that's fine. But if they park themselves in front of the TV and watch ten hours of *The Cosby Show*, that's not fine, because it's just too much TV at one time. And if they park themselves in front of the TV and watch thirty minutes of a very violent show, that's not fine at all.

"The Baby-sitters Club was made into videos. They're wholesome. They present nice values and introduce kids to things like volunteerism. But I don't want to see any kid parked in front of the TV watching the Baby-sitters Club for ten hours and not doing anything else. That's a big waste of time."

The first movie Ann ever saw was *101 Dalmations* — or 1001 Dalmations, as she called it at the time. Her Uncle Rick took her, and she loved it. The first movie her parents took her to see was *The Swiss Family Robinson*, so that's her official first movie. It's a big, wild adventure. (Or at least as big and wild as things got back then. Steven Spielberg and George Lucas weren't making movies yet.) Actually, Ann was a little bored. In the middle of the most exciting, action-packed scene, she leaned over and said, "Daddy, what does E-X-I-T spell?"

Actually, Ann still doesn't like action movies too much. They just don't interest her. Same with science fiction movies. She enjoys realistic movies more.

Ann loves comedies — of course — but not slapstick. She likes the witty comedies of Steve Martin and the other *Saturday Night Live*rs. She adores old-time, classic movies with the great actors of the past like Judy Garland, Fred Astaire, and Ginger Rogers. (She's crazy over the Astaire-Rogers classic, *Top Hat*, especially the dancing scenes.) Her two all-time favorites are *To Kill a Mockingbird* and *The Wizard of Oz*.

The worst kind of movies for Ann are the ones with a lot of violence in them. Those she never sees. Tough guy movies usually fall into this category. She does like scary movies, though not the really gory horror movies like *Halloween* or *Nightmare on Elm Street*. She prefers the psychological thrillers that really give you bad dreams! She sees most of the Stephen King movies and reads most of his books. She thinks King is a wonderful storyteller, and knows how to keep the reader enthralled.

Ann's musical tastes come mostly from her parents, who raised her and Jane on show tunes, big band and jazz music, and classical symphonies and chamber music. Ann and Jane did listen to rock, but weren't fanatical about it. The Martin parents feel lucky that they weren't blasted out of their house by a lot of loud rock and roll music when the girls were teenagers. (A lot of the other parents on the street were.) In high school, Ann's record collection included a lot of 45s of the Beatles and other popular groups. She owned many of the comedy records of Bill Cosby and George Carlin as well.

Ann still listens to show tunes and big band music. Often, she flips on the radio when she's doing chores or reading her mail. She likes the oldies and classic rock stations best. But she never, ever listens to music when she's writing. For that she needs absolute silence.

14
Volunteer!

Volunteering was a value the Martin parents taught their daughters. Mrs. Martin had always done a lot of community work. She volunteered at the hospital for 3500 hours. (That's thirty-five *hundred* hours.) The hospital issued little pins for every five or ten years you worked there, and they practically ran out of pins for Edie Martin.

Mr. Martin also used to help out at the hospital, usually by working on the annual fête. Once, he created sixteen full-sized cardboard horses to be used as decorations for a benefit dinner. He painted them intricately, like carousel horses.

The Martins always sponsored children through the Foster Parents Plan. The children lived in poor towns in foreign countries. The Martins would send a donation each month to the Foster Parents Plan, and the organization would use it and money from other foster parents to improve the town. They'd set up health clinics, dig new wells, or build water purification systems. The Foster Parents Plan benefited the entire town.

The Martins also wrote a letter each month to their foster children. Ann especially remembers Eleni Papadimitriou, who lived in a small town in Greece with her mother and older sister. Ann exchanged pictures with her and the Martins sent her Christmas and birthday cards.

The Martin parents were also animal lovers, and they were very involved with the Small Animal Veterinary Endowment (SAVE). That group took in and cared for stray animals. Mr. Martin helped SAVE start an animal shelter. He also designed their logo, which is a circle with a hand inside it holding a puppy and a kitten.

Ann became devoted to her own volunteer activities at an early age. She started as a candy striper at Princeton Hospital when she was fifteen. Mostly, she worked at Merwick, which was a nursing home. Ann would talk with the patients, arrange flowers visitors had brought, and help the nurses. Sometimes she'd take one of the patients for a walk on the hospital grounds. Or she'd push someone in a wheelchair. She *loved* it. It was wonderful to be able to bring comfort and pleasure to people through such simple actions. Some of the scenes from *Karen's Grandmothers,* in which Karen's class visits senior citizens in a home, are based on experiences Ann had at Merwick.

Ann also helped out in her mother's preschool

classroom when she had a day off from school. It was especially exciting because Ann wanted to be a teacher herself someday. Of course, she was a wonderful teacher's helper.

Ann and her friend Nancy were part of the Red Cross Youth Group. They helped raise money through bake sales and other activities. Through the Red Cross, Ann and Nancy ended up volunteering at a summer day camp for developmentally disabled children. They helped teach the kids arts and crafts, took them swimming, organized games, and went on group walks. It was Ann's first experience working with children with special needs, and she realized she had a natural ability with them.

Ann really hit her stride when she began working at Eden Institute, which is a school for autistic kids. Autism isn't a disease. There's nothing physically wrong with people who suffer from it. But autistic children don't know how to relate to the outside world. They can't communicate. Many of them do not talk. They may act strangely, make funny sounds, or even do things like eat gravel (this is what James does in Ann's book, *Inside Out*). In a way, the outside world just doesn't exist for autistic people.

Ann explains autism by saying, "These children are probably born with complete use of normal mental faculties, but they're so locked inside themselves that they have no way to communicate. I sometimes wonder why that happens, and what it must feel like to be bright and have no way to communicate."

Autism made the kids at Eden hard to bond with, but Ann loved the challenge. She remembers many of the children and their families, and has described a family like theirs in *Inside Out*. *Kristy and the Secret of Susan* is also based on some of Ann's experiences at Eden.

Ann spent the four summers during high school teaching at Eden Institute. For the first summer or two, she just helped the regular teachers wherever they needed her. But by the third and fourth summers, she was assigned one or two children to work with closely on her own.

Ann was responsible for creating an individualized lesson plan for each child. She might help the younger ones learn to wash their hands. The older kids would learn to dress. Some were learning to read and write. Mostly, Ann reinforced what the kids had learned over the year, because it was very easy for them to slip back and forget.

The summer consisted of many field trips and visits to local parks. Eden prides itself on teaching all its students to swim. They often took the kids to the Princeton pool. Sometimes, people would stare.

David Holmes, the director of Eden Institute, says, "Ann played a very important role because as a member of the Princeton community, she showed the rest of the people of the town that she cared about these kids and that she thought they had a right to be in the pool and in the community. She was making a real statement that way."

Working at Eden could mean dealing with a crisis every five minutes. Some of the kids would try to hurt themselves. Then the teachers would have to hold them until they calmed down. Ann might have to wrap her arms and even her legs around children to keep them from banging their heads against the wall or biting themselves.

When David Holmes first met Ann, he wasn't sure she could handle this part of the work — she was so gentle and quiet. But, he says, "Ann absolutely amazed not only me but the rest of my senior staff with the way she was able to jump in and just put all of her energy and spirit behind trying to help these little ones. It was absolutely flabbergasting."

At first, Ann was paid nothing. Later, though, she did receive a small salary — but it was so little she might as well have been working for free. She was dedicated to the work. She wasn't in it for the money.

The school was tiny when Ann started there. Over the years, it grew tremendously. Now, it is highly respected all over the nation. Ann helped to publicize the problems of families with autistic children in *Inside Out*. She dedicated the book to the kids at Eden Institute. Ann is still very devoted to the school and donates money to it every year.

Jane Martin also did and continues to do a lot of volunteer work. She took Mr. Reynolds, who was blind, shopping once a week when she was in high school. She spent time with boys in a juvenile home after school. She and her friends in the Interact Club would sponsor car washes and bake sales to raise money for social service agencies. Today, she serves food at a local soup kitchen in New York City. She volunteers at a hospital for kids with cancer. She also helps out at the 52nd Street Project, which teaches playwrighting and acting to inner city kids.

Ann continues to be involved with good works as an adult. Recently, she started her own foundation called, naturally, the Ann M. Martin Foundation. It makes donations to groups that help homeless people, educational programs, and kids. The foundation has helped to build a school in a small town in Ghana, West Africa, offered scholarships to poor children, and funded reading classes for adults, among other things.

Ann also started the Lisa Libraries with her friend Margot (that's me). The group encourages publishers to donate new children's books to them and these are then sorted into small libraries and passed on to after-school programs, homeless shelters, literacy programs, and community groups. The Lisa Libraries was started in memory of Lisa Novak, a friend and children's book editor who died in 1990.

Ann has also become involved with P.S. 2 in New York. Through Jacques d'Amboise's National Dance Institute she sponsors a dance program there, and some Baby-sitters Club readers who go to school have started a fan club. Ann speaks to

Ann visits with students at P.S. 2.

the club, which has since been transformed into a reading and writing group. She was glad to help the kids learn about the many wonderful authors who have inspired her.

Ann hopes to spread the idea of volunteering to her readers through her books. In *Jessi's Wish,* the Baby-sitters take a month off from sitting in order to volunteer. Helping others was a value Ann grew up with. No one told her she had to do it. She chose to.

Ann on Volunteering

"I think a lot of kids are interested in helping others and in volunteering, if I can believe what I read in the letters they write me. They want to find out how to be involved in their communities.

"Becoming involved is a wonderful way to stretch a little bit, to take a look around and see what else is out there. Finding that other people need help or caretaking, puts your own life into perspective."

15
College

When Ann was choosing colleges, she was terribly worried that she wouldn't get in to the ones she wanted to attend. Sure, she had great grades and glowing report cards. But she didn't test very well and her college board scores were only so-so. She applied to a number of easier colleges. Then, just hoping to get lucky, she sent applications to Smith College and Mount Holyoke College. Ann got in to every school she applied to. She was ecstatic when the acceptance from Smith arrived.

Smith is an all-women's school. It's set in a beautiful, green valley in the charming town of Northampton, Massachusetts. The red brick buildings and wooden houses are covered with ivy in the summer, and snow in the cold, blustery winters. It is a tough school, known for its fine teachers. It is definitely not a party school. The accent is on studying.

Attending an all-women's college was a good choice for a shy young woman like Ann. Ann's close friend from those years, Kate Durbin, describes it by saying, "Going to an all-women's school gave us all a stronger sense of community and it gave us time to grow up. But it could also sort of be like repeating sixth grade. Sometimes, we acted like twelve-year-old girls."

Smith is part of the Five Colleges. Buses connect Smith with four other schools, three of which are co-ed. So there were always plenty of guys around. Smith hosted mixers and parties. Guys from the other schools could take classes on campus. Ann and her friends enjoyed all the positive points of a women's school without being cut off from dating possibilities.

It isn't too surprising to learn that Ann continued to work extremely hard in college. Her favorite classes were education and psychology — which were her two majors. Fulfilling two majors was hard work, but both subjects were both so important to Ann that it was worth it. As part of her education major, Ann did her first practice teaching. She taught at the Smith College Campus School, an elementary school. She spent one semester with the preschool class and another with kindergarten kids. She loved it.

It was through her education courses that Ann began to read kids' books again. She took a course in children's literature. She used kids' books in the classes she taught. She began to read kids' books every spare moment she could. She even kept a file on them. The file included an outline of each story she read, a description of the illustrations, and a few words on how the book could be used in the classroom — for example, if it could help kids understand about divorce or learn how to get over a fight with a friend. And Ann wasn't planning to go into publishing or become a children's author at the time!

Ann kept up the file system both in college and after she had graduated. Of course, it came in very handy when she decided to go into publishing. She had already done major research on who was writing what and how good each book was.

In college, Ann took French for one more year (she'd been studying it since third grade). She loved that course because they read the great French comic dramatist, Molière, and Ann adored anything humorous. She also took Spanish for a year.

It was in college that Ann had a run-in with a truly terrible teacher — and it was in one of her favorite subjects, art. Ann just couldn't stand this teacher — and the teacher didn't seem to like her much either. The assignments were incredibly boring — at least to Ann. For the first few classes, the teacher brought in cardboard boxes and piled them up on a table in the center of the room. Drawing them was a good exercise in figuring out angles, lines, and perspective, but the assignment became very tedious.

Ann says, "A good teacher makes a good class. No matter how much you love a subject, if you have a horrible teacher, or if the teacher is horrible to *you*, you're not going to love that particular class."

Baby-sitters Club readers may remember something similar happening in *New York, New York!* In it, Mallory decides she must just have a very different idea than her teacher does of what art is. Claudia, on the other hand, does just fine in the class. A teacher can be good for one person and awful for another.

This art class was the only one, in the history of Ann's schooling, that she cut. She missed about half the drawing sessions, and got a C for the course. It was the lowest grade she ever got. Unfortunately, the class killed her interest in art lessons and she never took another course.

Most of Ann's close college friends lived in her dorm, or residence hall, which was called Gardiner House. Gardiner was one of the largest halls at Smith. It housed sixty women, which meant that people didn't know each other's business as much as they did in the smaller houses. That was nice for a private person like Ann. She could do her work, see her friends, and live her life without someone nosy or interfering.

Ann's room was very neat and well organized. She posted photos of her family on the walls. And she had a lot of children's books on her shelf. Her friend Claudia remembers the Beatrix Potter books and little ceramic figurines shaped like Peter Rabbit and the other Potter characters.

Ann met Kate Durbin because she was Ann's next door neighbor. She was a year ahead of Ann in school. Kate says her first impression of Ann was that she was "quiet, funny, and definitely someone worth getting to know." The real ice breaker came when Kate mentioned that she was from Louisville, Kentucky. Most of Ann's relatives lived there, and the two girls spent some time playing "Do-you-know . . ." They were friendly for the first few months of school, but became close during second semester.

Claudia Werner also lived in Gardiner House.

Ann and Claudia pose outside Gardiner House at Smith College. Now they've been friends for nearly two decades.

Claudia was a freshman. In fact, she and Ann were the only two freshmen on a hall of upper-classmen, and that brought them together quickly.

Soon, Ann had become part of a warm, close-knit group of women, most of whom were a year or two older than she was. They included Cary McMullen, Katina Metzidakis, Linda Crosby, Karen Brown, and a few others, in addition to Kate and Claudia. Ann had other friends, too, but the group of girls from Gardiner formed her core social circle and support system.

Claudia describes their friendship by saying, "I can tell Ann anything, and I don't feel that she would be judgmental. I can share things with her that I couldn't share with anyone else. We've gone through difficult times together. I know she's there. She's always been a really good listener. And we've always had a lot of fun together."

The group was mostly made up of homebodies. They ate a buffet lunch and a sit-down dinner together at Gardiner each day. Usually, they'd bring their books down with them to dinner so they could run right to the library after eating. They didn't want to waste the time to return to their rooms for books.

Claudia reports that, "Ann was the standard that we all tried to live up to as far as studying went. We had a core of really good, disciplined studiers. We all used to go traipsing off to the library every single night after dinner. Ann was sort of central to that. She wasn't trying to influence everybody, but she was just a good example."

Ann's friends were not the girls who went to every mixer on campus, or spent their weekends away. Instead, they spent long hours studying. On the weekends, they usually didn't get back from the library until 11:30 or midnight, and they'd all feel fairly silly. They'd get into their long, flannel Lanz nightgowns, which were the unofficial uniform of the group. They'd order pizzas or subs and watch *Saturday Night Live* on the TV in the dorm's communal living room.

If they felt truly wicked, they would all chip in and buy a half gallon of ice cream from Friendly's. They'd call a taxi company and the driver would pick it up for them. Then, one of them would run downstairs in her nightgown and pay the driver for the ice cream and the fare. It was the perfect snack for watching those reruns of the horror film, *The Exorcist*, which was a favorite. Each of them had memorized certain lines, which they'd call out at the appropriate moment.

Mostly, though, the girls didn't watch much television. For a while, Kate was the only one who owned her own set, and it was an old, cast-off black-and-white from her grandmother. They preferred each other's company over the TV.

Conversations revolved around things like family or roommates or boyfriends on distant campuses. Claudia remembers that Ann talked a lot about her cousins and grandmother. The girls all had different majors, so they didn't tend to discuss schoolwork. Nevertheless, it was a supportive group of friends. Says Kate, "We were all good listeners. It was a very tight circle in terms of emotional support. But we all shared the same silly sense of humor. We had a lot of fun."

One night, the girls were sitting around in the hallway, and somehow they began making up fake names for each other. These were supposed to be their pen names when they became famous authors — though none of them, not even Ann, intended to be a writer at the time. Claudia dubbed Ann Fern Nesbitt. (She confides that she's really a little disappointed that Ann has never published anything under the name.) Kate was Bunny. Claudia became Desiree Sinclair. They were only teasing, but the nicknames stuck. Kate still sometimes writes a note or makes a phone call to Fern. And Claudia's kids call Ann Auntie Fern.

Kate says, "Particularly for Ann, who worked so hard and felt so much pressure to do well, it was a real respite to just relax and be silly for a while."

Every Sunday, the girls would eat breakfast at Burger King. It may not sound very fancy, but when you're stuck on a college campus with piles of reading to do, even simple things can be exciting. Afterward, they might go shopping, hang out in each other's rooms or, most likely, hit the library. They might take in a movie in town or on campus. In the winter, there was ice skating on the pond. Says Ann, "Unless you looked hard, there wasn't a lot to do in that town."

From time to time, the group would visit Katina's brother or Claudia's boyfriend at Yale University, and meet their friends. Ann did join them, but not often. She felt too much pressure about her work. Kate explains, "Ann really took college seriously. From day one, she was there to get straight A's, and that's why she graduated with honors. She worked very hard for it."

Aside from studying and hanging out with her friends, Ann volunteered at the state mental institution not far from the campus. There, she tutored some of the patients. And she taught sewing at an after-school program in town.

One of the big events at Smith each fall was Mountain Day. One fine, crisp morning in September or October, the president of the college would ring the college bells. That meant all classes were canceled, and everyone was supposed to drop what they were doing and take the day off. The students would bike, hoof it, or drive off for a day in the country. The dining halls would pack picnic lunches for them.

The leaves would just be starting to turn. The apple orchards would be ripe with fruit. Having an unexpected day off was exhilarating. Ann and her friends used to pedal their bikes into the country. Sometimes, though, Ann would stay behind and use the day to catch up on her schoolwork. The most studious of the Smith girls did tend to do that.

In the spring, an important event was Parents' Weekend. Parents would arrive, and they and their daughters would go to special lectures, art exhibits, concerts, and movies. Ann and her friends would eat dinner out in groups with their parents. It was fun to get to know everybody's mother and father.

Usually, summer vacation meant returning to Princeton to work at Eden, and maybe taking a vacation with the family. One summer, though, Ann and Kate drove to Louisville together. Kate had a huge Chrysler, which the girls had dubbed Quasimodo (or simply Quasi), after the main character in Victor Hugo's classic novel *The Hunchback of Notre Dame*. Kate was used to driving this monster car. But Ann was nervous. She didn't love driving to begin with, and she'd never been behind the wheel of something so big. But she buckled down — and buckled *up* — and did it. Kate says she was a real trooper about it.

In between the first and second semester of the year at Smith, was a month-long break called Interterm. Each Smith student had to design and complete an independent study project. For her freshman Interterm, Ann went back to Princeton to teach at Eden Institute. Senior year, she spent Interterm writing her two huge thesis papers, one for each of her majors. Each one was approximately fifty pages long. Ann's education paper was about using children's literature in the classroom. Later, her father had it bound. For her psychology paper, Ann wrote about the effects of TV violence on kids.

Ann's last year of school was lonely. Most of her friends were a year older than she was, and they'd graduated and moved away. Claudia had gotten married and was finishing school in Texas. Of course, Ann had other friends and a lot of work to keep her busy. She wrote letters to her graduate friends — everyone was too broke for big phone bills. The girls sent newspaper clippings and funny cartoons with the letters. They signed off with various clever and silly names, like Molly Coddle, Natalie Attired, and Mary Maker.

Ann graduated from college in 1977, with honors. She had accomplished everything she had set out to do when she'd arrived at Smith four years earlier.

Though the girls from Gardiner House are now scattered across the country, they remain in touch. Ann is particularly close with Kate, Claudia, and Cary. They show up as bridesmaids in each other's

In 1984, the Smith friends reunited at a baby shower for Katina. From left to right, that's Kate (who was expecting Claire at the time), Cary, Linda, Ann, Claudia, and Katina.

124

wedding photos. They have long telephone conversations. And they visit each other whenever they can.

Recently, Claudia made a special trip to New York to stay with Ann. She was studying for her medical specialty boards, and she knew she'd need to concentrate very hard on what she was doing. She wanted to get back to the discipline and single-mindedness of her college study sessions. And she knew Ann's was the perfect place to do it. After all, Ann had always been her best study partner back in college.

So Claudia took six days off from her job and family and went to New York. She said nothing had changed. She'd work all day, while Ann worked on a Baby-sitters Club book. At the end of each day, they went out for pizza and had some great late-night talks. And Claudia passed her exam.

Ann has become important in the lives of her friends' children. She is the godmother of Kate's son, Andrew, and she's close with Kate's daughter, Claire. Ann and Claire (a devoted BSC fan) write letters and talk on the phone often. Kate says Ann is extraordinarily attentive. She sends not only birthday and Christmas presents, but Halloween presents (things like funny flashlights, or pumpkin tights) and Easter toys. Claire always gets a copy of the newest Baby-sitters Club and Little Sister books, and any Baby-sitters Club clothes or toys that come out. Kate and Claire sometimes visit Ann in New York. They might go to the circus or a

Ann and Kate playing dress-up with Claire, age four. Claire is wearing a dress made by Ann.

Broadway show, or play on the big *Alice in Wonderland* statue in Central Park.

Ann is also the godmother of Claudia's daughter, Rachel (whom everyone calles Rachie). Rachie is still too little for outings with Ann, but Ann has flown to Dallas for Rachie's birthday and, of course, she is always making clothes for her.

Says Kate, "Building a trust and a comfort level takes time for Ann — and then it's there forever. If I fell off the face of the earth today, I could call Ann up in fifteen years and it would be as though nothing had ever happened."

16
Careers

Ann always wanted to be a teacher. It was the only career she ever considered as a child. And everyone just assumed that's what she *would* be. Sure, they knew she loved to write. But it was just a fun hobby. No one expected her to become an author.

Well, at least her family and friends didn't. Some of her teachers had an idea that things might turn out differently. Ann's fourth-grade teacher, Mrs. Dreeben, says, "Ann always loved writing. I noted in her folder that in adulthood she could be a writer if she wanted. There was no question in any of the teachers' minds. She spent a lot of her free time doing her own writing, and what she wrote was beautiful."

But for her early years and all the way through college, Ann kept very quiet about her interest in writing. Kate reports that Ann did send manuscripts for a few picture books to publishers during college, but they were not accepted. Of course, Ann was disappointed — who wouldn't be — but she never made a big deal about it.

What she talked about and worked hardest at was becoming a teacher. Though Ann hadn't always been so happy at school herself, she loved working with kids. She hoped that as a teacher, she might be able to create a better way to do things than she'd experienced herself in school.

Ann got some of her first teaching experience as a baby-sitter. She wasn't the kind of sitter who watched TV all afternoon with her charges. She always tried to engage the kids in fun activities — things they could both enjoy and learn from. Assisting with her mother's classes and working as a practice teacher in college gave her other valuable teaching experience.

When Ann graduated from Smith College, she had already lined up a teaching job. It was at a small school in Connecticut that served elementary school-aged children, most of whom were special in some way. Some were mildly developmentally disabled. Some were behind in school because they'd had serious illnesses and had missed a year. Others were gifted. Yet others were dyslexic. She chose that school because she had enjoyed working with special kids at Eden Institute and at the summer camp for developmentally disabled children.

Ann co-taught a class of fourth- and fifth-graders. She loved teaching and living on her own. The town wasn't far from New Jersey, so she could visit her family whenever she wanted. Kate and Karen, from college, were both living nearby, and Ann stayed in contact with them.

And if Ann was worried about making friends in a new place, that never became a problem. She met some wonderful people the day she moved into her new apartment. She also became close with some of the other teachers at the school. She has remained friends with several of them over the years. When Pam and Jim Fulton had their twin sons, Andrew and Patrick, they asked Ann to be baby Andrew's godmother. The family comes to visit Ann in New York. Andrew loved *Disney on Ice* when Ann took him a few years ago. They've also been to the circus, the American Museum of Natural History, and Central Park.

Ann had always been interested in writing, but had never considered it as a career. Her work as a teacher, though, began to make her think more seriously about it. She used a lot of wonderful books for children in her classroom. She had always loved kids' books, and began to consider writing some herself.

After the first year of teaching, Ann decided to leave the school where she was working. She wanted to teach in a different kind of school. But by the time she made up her mind to do it, the school year was nearly over. She was sure she wouldn't be able to get another teaching job by the fall. So she looked for a job in a different field, until she could find another school where she could teach. That field was children's publishing.

New York City is the place to be if you're working in publishing, and that is where all of Ann's editorial jobs have been. At first, she moved back to her parents' house and commuted to the city. After a while, she moved in with Karen, who had gotten an apartment in New York with a roommate. A lot of Ann's other friends lived in the city as well. She saw Kate often. They worked across the street from each other for a few years, and would get together for lunch or an after-work snack.

Ann began as an editorial assistant and worked her way up to senior editor. She spent six years at some of the best-known publishing houses in New York City. She loved being involved with kids' books, no matter what she had to do. She enjoyed everything from coming up with ideas and reading manuscripts right down to typing a memo. The only thing she wasn't excited about was going over writers' contracts. Ann was interested in the creative side of publishing, not the business side.

Being an editor made Ann think more and more about actually writing herself. She saw so many different manuscripts pass through her office, that she sometimes thought she could write one just as well. In 1980, she began working on her first book, which was called *Bummer Summer*.

Ann took only one writing class in college, because she was too busy with her required courses. She says she learned most of what she knows

Ann on Writing

"One interesting thing about writing is that when you're making up a story, you're in charge. You can solve problems the way you wish they could be solved in real life. It's a way to work out the 'if onlys' and the 'what ifs.' The 'if onlys' are all the things you think about, all the solutions to problems in your own life that you didn't come up with fast enough. You know — when something happens in school and later that night you think, Oh, if only I had said this or that. Well, when you're writing, you can say or do those things.

"And the 'what ifs' are simply anything you can imagine. You can have fun playing out all those scenes and situations you might like to see happen in real life — and things you wouldn't like to see happen, as well. The 'what ifs' are your creative mind at work."

about writing from reading other authors, and from editing manuscripts.

It took Ann about a year and a half to finish a first draft of the book, because she could only work on it early in the morning before work and on weekends. When it was done, she gave it to a friend, who gave it to another friend, who gave it to a third friend who worked at a literary agency. That woman was Amy Berkower, now one of the best children's book agents in the business. But at the time, Amy was just starting out as well. Amy liked *Bummer Summer* and sent it to two publishing houses. It was rejected at both places.

But at the third place, Holiday House, a new young editor named Margery Cuyler showed some interest. She didn't think the book was perfect, though, and began working with Ann to make some changes. After another year and a half, the manuscript had been re-written. However, Margery couldn't promise to publish the book because the company was interested in two other new books, and they could pick only one of three.

It was quite extraordinary of Margery to work with Ann. Usually, a publisher simply accepts a book or rejects it, *before* working with a new author. But Margery worked hard with Ann on *Bummer Summer*. She believed in it. In the end, Holiday House chose to publish *Bummer Summer*, and Ann's career as a professional writer began.

For the next few years, Ann continued to work as an editor. She was afraid she couldn't make a living writing, and she wanted the security of a steady job. She wrote four more books in that time — *Inside Out*, a story taken from her years teaching at Eden Institute; *Stage Fright*, which was loosely based on her own fear of performing in front of crowds; *Me and Katie (the Pest)*, which is a heightened version of her childhood fights with Jane (Ann's riding lessons also play a part in that book); and *With You and Without You*, which is about a young girl whose father dies. She wrote all these books in the mornings before she went to her regular job and on weekends. Ann's books

The publicity photo, taken by Jane, from the jacket of Bummer Summer.

were well received. They earned very nice reviews. *Bummer Summer* even made the Children's Choice List.

After a while, it became clear that Ann just wouldn't have time to do all the writing she wanted and still work a regular job. She thought long and hard about a change. At last, she was ready to take the plunge. She decided to leave her job at Bantam Books and write full-time.

It was a difficult step to take. She was giving up a sure thing for something unknown and uncertain. Says Kate, "I really admire Ann. In a lot of ways, she would strike people as timid and not able to take the kind of risk that would allow her to quit her job — forget a regular paycheck and a pension and just do it. There's a great deal of strength inside her."

In preparation for the big change, Ann slowly saved money. She signed up as much work as she could before giving notice at her job. Luckily, she was well connected in the publishing world. A lot of people knew that she was hardworking and dependable.

Being a free-lance writer takes discipline. If you work a regular job, you know you have to wake up each morning and be on time or your boss will get mad. But free-lancers have to set the alarm and get up all on their own. And once you're up, there's always the temptation of an *I Love Lucy* rerun or some other show you convince yourself you just can't miss.

Luckily, Ann has a strong sense of discipline. She'd had a wonderful example of a disciplined free-lancer in her father, who woke up earlier than many other fathers to go to his studio and draw all day long. She'd practiced discipline as well with her rigid study schedule in college. She was ready to go.

Ann liked the change from working in an office to working in her home. In an office, there are forms to fill out and procedures to follow. Ann sometimes spent more time in meetings than actually working with books. At home, Ann could be her own boss.

In the beginning, Ann wrote just about everything anyone would hire her to do. She helped write a few books for other people's series. She wrote novelizations of movies. She found as much free-lance editing work as she could. And she did well. She never lacked for work, and she made enough money. But, like many authors, she often worried that each project would be her last. The work would stop. She'd be unemployed.

She shouldn't have worried. She had already spoken to Jean Feiwel. Jean was then an editorial director at Scholastic, she'd worked with Ann before, and she had a great idea for a new series. It would be about a group of girls who did a lot of baby-sitting, and it would be called the Baby-sitters Club. The series would start with just four books. She wanted Ann to write them. Ann agreed, and the rest is history.

17
The Birth of a Super Series

Claudia, Stacey, Mary Anne, and Kristy — the girls who
started a movement.

The first Baby-sitters Club book was published on August 1, 1986. Ann dedicated that book to Beth Perkins, the real-life model for Kristy.

The idea for the series was Jean Feiwel's. But Jean is not a writer herself. She had to find someone creative, professional, and fun to create the characters and stories and write the books. She thought of Ann immediately.

Ann and Jean had worked together at Scholastic a few years earlier. Jean had read Ann's books and thought they were good. She knew that Ann was hardworking and could produce high-quality books quickly and efficiently. Jean thought Ann understood what writing for children was all about. And she liked working with her.

But what Jean didn't know was that she was hiring just about the best baby-sitter in the whole world to write the series. That was a lucky coincidence.

Ann was thrilled to get the job. She was a new writer at the time, and signing up a four-book series was big news. It also assured her that she'd be working for at least a year. She'd be able to pay her bills without worrying. She was also very excited about working on a series about baby-sitting because she'd enjoyed sitting so much herself.

Jean thought the series would do well. She hoped that the original four-book series might be expanded to eight or even twelve stories. She had no way of guessing that eventually the series would sell millions of copies each year. She couldn't have realized that every single one of the

Baby-sitters Club titles would make the best-seller list, with most of them reaching the number-one spot. Today, the Baby-sitters Club books are available in thirteen languages and fifteen foreign countries.

After the Baby-sitters Club books became successful, Ann and Jean came up with the idea for the Little Sister series. They hoped they could have two hit series instead of one — and they do!

Jean explains that, "The Little Sister series evolved because Ann was completely smitten with Karen. Karen was always a shining light in the Baby-sitters Club series. She came to life fully formed and talking too loudly. She was just very strong. When you develop lesser characters, sometimes they stay in the background for a few books until they come into their own. Karen was somebody who just leapt out. From the very beginning, Ann had a very clear picture of exactly who she was."

Ann adds, "Karen is my alter ego. She's who I wish I could be. She is a true character."

Jean couldn't be more pleased with her choice of author. She says that Ann has remained as diligent as ever over the many years of hard work. She has never let her success make her sloppy. She wants every single book to be just as good as the last one, and she's willing to put in the time and energy to make it happen. She also says that Ann gives an awful lot back to the Scholastic staff on a personal level. She remembers everybody's birthday, and never forgets to ask about family.

Jean and Ann have gotten to know each other extremely well through their work. They have both brought many personal experiences and strongly held beliefs to the series. You can't work that closely with someone without learning a great deal about what's inside her. Ann and Jean have become close friends.

Making a book involves many people besides the author. Producing two best-selling books per month takes an incredible amount of effort. It involves all the people who work in the Scholastic art and publicity departments, the editors and copy editors, the printers, the book distributors, and many more. And then there's Bethany Buck, the series editor. A different editor, Brenda Bowen, worked with Ann on the first twenty books. When she left Scholastic, Bethany took her place as editor of the Baby-sitters Club. Bethany, like Brenda before her, is responsible for coordinating all the people involved with creating and publishing the books. She also edits every one of the Baby-sitters Club and Little Sister books, with some help.

Here is how a Baby-sitters Club story goes from a starting idea to the finished book which you hold in your hand: First, Ann and her publisher sign a contract for all the books for the coming year, including regular books, Super Specials, and other releases.

Then, Ann sits down with Jean and Bethany and they discuss each book. Usually, they go to lunch at a little restaurant near the Scholastic offices on Broadway. It's always a *very* long lunch. The Baby-sitters Club masterminds also have a second long lunch meeting about the Little Sister series.

After that, Ann gets to work. She writes a complete outline — about twenty pages — of everything that will happen in each book. She pieces together ideas, plot twists, and fun events like holidays, trips, and school activities. Ann has deadlines for each outline, and she is very, very careful never to be late.

Once the outline is finished, she and Bethany go over the story *again*. They make some changes. And at last, the book is ready to be written. Ann sits down in her office, which is a quiet room in her apartment, with a pad of paper and a pen.

If Ann is having trouble with something as she's writing, she might call Bethany and run an idea

The masterminds behind the Baby-sitters Club — Jean, Ann, and Bethany look at a painting for the cover of a BSC book.

by her. For instance, she might have forgotten Jessi's hamster's name. Or she may want to discuss whether Bethany thinks it's okay for Claudia to cheat on a test.

Though both Bethany and Ann are extremely serious about the books, they do joke around a lot as they work together. For instance, they might laughingly compare something in a book story line to something that happened on an *I Love Lucy* episode.

Ann has a *very* tight schedule. She wakes up at quarter of six each morning and is at her desk by 8:00 (8:30 at the latest). Ann's pace is probably faster than any other well-known kids' book author. One time, Ann went to a dinner party at a friend's house. The phone rang and Ann's friend joked, "Ann, it's your publisher. They need another book by ten o'clock tonight."

If Ann sticks to her schedule absolutely, she can take weekends off to see friends, relax, work on sewing projects, and read. But if she falls behind even one page, she has to make it up on the weekend. This makes Ann's life very pressured. She sometimes has to sacrifice doing fun things with her friends in order to do her best on every book.

Ann does all her writing in longhand, with a pad and pen. One of her assistants types everything Ann wrote the day before into a computer. Ann doesn't do too much work on the computer herself. She isn't very comfortable with complicated machines and mechanical devices. She likes to keep things simple.

After much work, and nervousness about making the deadline, the manuscript is finally finished. Ann sends it over to the Scholastic offices by messenger, or walks it over herself. (Scholastic isn't far from her home.)

Because Ann and Bethany have prepared so much for each story, Ann usually doesn't have to make many changes after she turns in a manuscript. Of course, there are always a few little slips or mistakes. For instance, in one Little Sister book, Kristy's family had bought a new van. But Bethany noticed that the van never showed up in the Baby-sitters Club books. Bethany makes these kinds of changes herself and Ann okays them later.

Although Bethany edits all the Baby-sitters Club and Little Sister books, Jean also works on any of the books that might be a little controversial or special. Those are the books that deal with more serious subjects, like when Jessi and Claudia faced racism or the time Jessi baby-sat for a little girl with cancer.

Then the manuscript goes to a copy editor. His or her job is to check for and correct mistakes. For instance, if Jackie Rodowsky is wearing a blue shirt at the beginning of a scene, he better not be wearing a green one at the end. And if this scene appears on the cover of the book, Jackie's shirt should be blue in the picture as well. The copy editor also checks the spelling and grammar. Ann is a great speller and has excellent grammar, but everyone makes mistakes sometimes.

You may wonder how Ann can possibly keep

up with so many books — more than two per month, every month. Well, she does have some help. Though she writes the majority of the material, some of the books are now written by other authors. They work from Ann's very detailed outlines, and when they're finished, Ann goes over each one. She changes sentences so that they sound the way *she* would write them. This is not because what the other writers write is bad. But it's Ann's series and she wants every book to be as close to the way she would have written it herself as possible. Ann does a tremendous amount of work on every book, even the ones that are written when she's on vacation. Each Baby-sitters Club and Little Sister book reflects Ann's vision and voice.

Everyone who works on the Baby-sitters Club series has her favorite types of stories. Ann enjoys the books that deal with serious issues the most — stories like *Jessi's Secret Language, Kristy and the Secret of Susan,* and *Claudia and the Sad Good-bye*. Jean's personal favorites are the tearjerkers and the romantic stories. She cried when she read *Kristy and the Snobs,* in which Kristy's family dog, Louie, dies. It reminded her of when her own dog died. Bethany tends to like the funny books such as *Little Miss Stoneybrook . . . and Dawn,* and *Boy-Crazy Stacey*.

No one should be too surprised to hear that Bethany thinks Ann is just great to work with. She takes care of as many details as possible herself, and she does a fantastic job. Ann is *always* on time.

In fact, Bethany can remember only two or three times when Ann was late with anything. With dozens of deadlines each year, that's pretty impressive. And of course, when Ann *was* late, she felt awful — even though she handed in her work within a day or two. She apologized and apologized. Ann hates being late so much that she'll take her work with her when she makes an author visit. She'll edit a manuscript on a plane, or read through a typeset version of the book.

Ann likes working with Jean and Bethany as well. It is very helpful to pass her ideas by them, and use some of their suggestions. She's quite certain that they know what they're doing when it comes to creating and publishing hit book series. She knows she can trust them.

When a BSC manuscript is finally finished it still has a long way to go before it is a book. Next comes production. This involves creating a cover, setting the story in print, manufacturing the book, and making sure it is distributed to the bookstores. Bethany coordinates the many pieces of production. She comes up with ideas for cover pictures and discusses them with David Tommasino, an art director at Scholastic, and his staff. Sometimes, she asks Ann for advice on covers.

Bethany finds details from the manuscript that will help the art department staff with the cover. She lets them know what the characters should be wearing and, if a new character is appearing, what type of personality he or she has. For instance, if the cover is supposed to feature a tough little girl, the model picked by the art staff shouldn't be a sweet, gentle-looking child.

The art department looks through modeling books in order to pick out the characters for the cover and sets up a photo shoot in a studio. Of course, the models who appear on the cover are used again and again until they outgrow their "parts"! A photographer then takes several rolls of film of, for instance, Kristy and Karen baking cookies, or whatever is featured in that particular story.

After that, an artist does a sketch from the photo. The artist who makes the Baby-sitters Club covers is a man named Hodges Soileau (pronounced Swallow) and the Little Sister covers are the creations of Susan Tang. Bethany looks at each sketch. She might ask the artist for some changes. For instance, she might want the earrings taken off of Kristy (Kristy doesn't have pierced ears) or she might want one of the charges to look a little younger. Once the sketch is okayed, the artist paints a picture from it. Hodges and Susan must make one painting or more each month to keep up with the book covers. It's a very fast pace.

Bethany writes cover copy for each book. That's the summary on the back of the book that makes you think it would probably be a good story to buy.

The Scholastic marketing department is in charge of the contests in the backs of the books for readers to enter. They ask Bethany for advice, too. For instance, they came up with the idea for Karen's birthday club. Readers could sign up to receive a postcard from Karen on their birthdays. Marketing asked Bethany if someone in one of the Little Sister books would be having a birthday soon. They wanted to coordinate the contest with a birthday book.

After all those stages of production, the book is ready to be printed and shipped to stores. Baby-sitters Club fans also buy Ann's series through book clubs and book fairs. A lot of work goes into making a series successful once it's in the stores. The marketing department must make sure Baby-sitters Club advertisements are just a little better than the ones for other books. And Ann does a lot of publicity. She has flown to dozens of states for lectures and signings at bookstores, libraries, and schools.

With the Baby-sitters Club and Little Sister series becoming so popular, a lot of merchandising has sprung up around the books. There are Baby-sitters Club backpacks and nightshirts, sleeping bags and cosmetics, dolls and stationery sets, games and jigsaw puzzles. Ann is involved with the planning of each item. She wants everything connected to the series to be of a very high quality. She sits down with toy company executives and clothing manufacturers and talks about how she'd like each item to look.

The Baby-sitters Club videos have also become very popular. Ann doesn't write the scripts, but she does discuss the plots with the screenwriters. She met the young actresses who were auditioning for parts in the videos, and helped pick which girls would get the parts. Bethany helped, too. They thought they'd found the perfect Mary Anne — but the actress wore braces, and Mary Anne doesn't. Eventually, the actress had her braces taken off so she could play the part!

At first, the videos were meant just for purchase at stores. But when HBO heard about them, they decided to air the videos, too.

People often ask Ann why she thinks her series has become so amazingly popular. She says, "The Baby-sitters Club was a lot of the right things coming together at the right time — a market that was ready for something like this, a company such as Scholastic that was willing to put everything possible behind something they believed in, and the right writer for the series. You know, even if all these things came together now, it might not be the right time. There weren't as many series to compete with when the Baby-sitters Club first came out. It really was luck."

18
The Real-Life
Baby-sitters Club

Though most of the characters in the Baby-sitters Club are made up, Ann's real-life experiences and friends do show up in the books. For example, Kristy and Mary Anne are loosely based on Beth and Ann.

Ann explains how she assembled the mixed cast of characters who people the books: "When I was coming up with the characters before the series began, I wanted a group of very different kids who all got along well together. Each would have her own sets of problems, which she could talk about with her friends. For instance, I decided one character would have a physical problem of some kind. I chose diabetes for Stacey because it's a fairly common problem with kids and it's something that takes a certain amount of management and control. I also know a few people who are diabetic."

Beth's family, the Perkinses (she and her husband and three daughters), are the only characters in the Baby-sitters Club who are real people outside of the series. Their pets, especially their dog, Chewbacca, also appear in the books. But as Baby-sitters Club fans know, time stands still in the series. Myriah was five when she first appeared in the books, and has remained that age throughout the series. In real life, though, she has grown up and is now in middle school. She has developed many interests that she didn't have when the series first started.

It doesn't matter to Myriah and her sisters that they're so young in the books. In fact, Myriah says she likes reading about her imaginary summer vacations and her many Christmases, all of which

Here's Ann with the Perkins' girls just weeks after Laura was born — shortly after the time they began appearing in the BSC books. In this picture, Myriah is six and Gabbie is three.

she has suppposedly had at the age of five! Gabbie Perkins says that being in the Baby-sitters Club has helped her make friends. One girl's friendly name for her is "Baby-sitter Girl."

In a way, Claudia Kishi and her sister Janine could be Ann and Jane, but only because they're two sisters who are so very different. Ann is hardly a genius, like Janine, and Jane never had as much trouble in school as Claudia. Ann took her and Jane's situation and heightened it.

Ann says, "I probably hear my parents' voices in the back of my head when I'm writing about most parents. They are the model for everything from the way a parent handles a crisis to the way he or she deals with a kid who's not eating dinner."

Of course, not every family in the Baby-sitters Club series is based on Ann's own sister and parents. Ann explains. "I like to show different kinds of families in my books. A family doesn't have to be a mom and a dad and a brother and a sister. It can be extended, like Kristy's, or it can be like Stacey's and Dawn's, in which part of the family lives in one city and the other part lives far away, maybe even across the country. For instance, when Stacey is in Connecticut, her family consists of just her and her mom, and that's as much of a family as Claudia and her sister and her mother and father and grandmother, when Mimi was alive."

Of course, a number of books come directly from

Ann's personal experiences. The book *Kristy and the Baby Parade* is based on a real baby parade, complete with floats and wild outfits, which was held each year in Avalon.

The idea for *Jessi's Wish* came from Ann's involvement with two real organizations called the Make-a-Wish Foundation and the Starlight Foundation. They appear in the book as an organization called Your Wish Is My Command. Like the imaginary organization in the book, they grant requests to kids who are sick with life-threatening illnesses. The Starlight Foundation first contacted Ann when one child, a Baby-sitters Club fan, asked for a visit from her favorite author. Ann was honored to help grant the little girl's wish. She has made other contributions and donations to both Starlight and Make-a-Wish. She also made sure part of the proceeds from *Jessi's Wish* went to support Make-a-Wish.

Claudia and the Phantom Phone Calls is about the girls getting some frightening phone calls. They invent a telephone code to alert their friends if they're in trouble. This is something Ann and Beth did together when they were baby-sitters. Luckily, they never needed to use their code.

As for *The Ghost at Dawn's House,* that secret passage is something Ann always wished she had in her own home. That probably came from all those Nancy Drew books she read!

Ann says, "Sometimes my personal interests leak into the books, even if I haven't really had a lot of experience with them. For whatever reason, I just happen to be fascinated by American Sign Language, which was why the character Matt Braddock was created. He's profoundly deaf. He has no speech and communicates solely with sign language. This was just interesting to me, and I hoped I could make it interesting to kids as well. And the same thing happened with *Kristy and the Worst Kid Ever*, which is about a family who takes in a foster child."

Other things from real life filter into the Baby-sitters Club books, but in a changed form. For instance, Ann picked the name Pike for Mallory's family because there was a large family named Pike living near her when she was growing up. But the real Pikes had six kids, not eight, and none of their characters is similar to any of the Pike kids in the books.

The term *silly-billy-goo-goo,* which Claire Pike uses when she's feeling silly, has an interesting story behind it. Ann explains: "I was walking down the street in New York one day and I passed a couple of kids who were about five years old. They were getting silly as only five-year-olds can get, and one of them called the other a silly-billy-goo-goo. They both practically fell down on the sidewalk from laughing so hard." Ann picked up the term, and it has become a part of the Baby-sitters Club universe.

When Ann speaks at schools, libraries, and bookstores she says kids question her about almost every single detail of the Baby-sitters Club books.

"Kids often ask why I picked a certain name for a certain character. In a way, it's like asking why I ate a certain thing for breakfast that morning. I just felt like it!" Many things about writing are just chance.

19
Success

Ann never ran after fame. She just wanted to live quietly and write her books, but something extraordinary happened to her along the way. Ann stresses that she's very lucky to have become as successful as she has. She says, "I think kids should realize that this is a sort of fairy tale, and that it doesn't happen to most people who set out to write books. There are many excellent writers who earn a nice living. But an awful lot of writers hold down a second job to support themselves. Something like this is really unusual and lucky."

Being part of the Baby-sitters Club family has brought many wonderful and exciting things into Ann's life. One of the best was when an eleven-year-old girl read *The Truth About Stacey* and diagnosed herself as having juvenile diabetes. She realized that her symptoms were the same as the ones Stacey experiences in the book. This happened just before Thanksgiving one year, and the doctors said later that if the girl had eaten a lot of sweets over the holiday, she could have ended up in a coma. In fact, she isn't the only child who read *The Truth About Stacey* and found out the truth about herself.

Many diabetic children have written to Ann saying that they feel more comfortable with their condition after reading the Baby-sitters Club books. The stories also help them explain their special diets and insulin injections to their friends. All they have to do is hand them the book and let them read about it.

Ann's success has allowed her to start the foundation mentioned earlier. Ann was inspired to start it because she felt that she was receiving so much from children all over the world who bought her books. She wanted to give something back, especially to the people who need it the most. Says Ann, "Starting the foundation was certainly one of the best things that's come of my success."

Becoming a well-known author has allowed Ann to meet dozens of wonderful people she probably never would have met otherwise. Some of them have been famous themselves. It's still a thrill for her to meet many of the authors she admires most, like Madeleine L'Engle, Patricia MacLachlan, and Mildred Taylor.

Other people Ann has enjoyed meeting are just "regular" folks. Sherry Lopez is a fan of Ann's from Brooklyn, who has become her friend.

Around Christmastime, they might get together for lunch, a shopping spree in a bookstore, and a whirlwind tour of the holiday windows on Fifth Avenue. In her early years as an author, Ann became pen pals with some of the first few readers ever to send her fan letters. Ann now receives about fifteen thousand letters each year. Of course, she can't be pen pals with all those children. And she can't take on any new pen pals. But she keeps up with the old ones. These girls, like Kathy Ames, are now some of Ann's younger friends. She sends them birthday presents and arranges for special New York days with them when they have a chance to visit. Ann attended Kathy's twelfth birthday party at Tavern on the Green, a fancy New York restaurant in Central Park. Ann also corre-

Ann helps Kathy Ames celebrate Kathy's twelfth birthday.

sponds with the three children she sponsors through Save the Children, and with youngsters she has met through the Make-A-Wish Foundation and the Starlight Foundation.

It was through Kathy Ames that Ann met children's author, Paula Danziger. Paula was addressing a middle-school class, and a number of the kids were curious about other famous writers she might know. Kathy raised her hand and asked if Paula had ever met Ann. Paula said she hadn't, but that Ann sounded nice from her books. Kathy said she was one of Ann's pen pals and suggested a meeting between the two authors. Then she wrote to Ann.

Not much later, Paula received a shy message from Ann on her telephone answering machine, wondering if they could get together. Paula thought, Well, why not? and the two met for dinner. They hit it off immediately, and have been close friends ever since. Paula says of Ann, "She has a real heart about things. She cares. She's a good friend to call when I'm having problems with dating, hair, clothing choices, and other world-shattering issues, like dust in my contact lenses. I can also count on her to call me when she's terrified of a spider she's found in her house, when her cats do something *she* thinks is funny, and when she wants to tell me about an *I Love Lucy* episode she's just seen for the eightieth time.

"Seriously . . . I've also learned a lot from Annie about helping others, and I'm very glad she's my friend (even at three in the morning when the spider shows up)."

Ann and Paula's friendship includes a large helping of silliness. One time, they bought a plastic kid's bank in the shape of a Brownie's head. They dubbed the bank Bob, and Ann proceeded to apply makeup to Bob's eyes and lips. Later, when Paula made a trip to Europe, Ann pretended Bob had been kidnapped. Phoney ransom notes followed Paula from country to country. The best one was accompanied by a package of pennies with a note from Ann that said simply, "Bob threw up!"

But beneath the silliness is a lot of nurturing and support between Ann and Paula. They share problems and pressures as well as jokes.

Ann isn't the kind of person who's interested in buying lots of expensive things. She doesn't get excited about boats and planes. Sure, it's nice to be able to buy a beautiful pair of earrings when she wants to. It's great not to have to worry about paying bills and to be able to afford luxuries. But the money is less important to her than knowing she is doing a fine job with her series.

Still, nice things do come to well-known authors, and Ann is very thankful for the many lovely things her success has brought into her life. A number of years ago, she bought a beautiful co-op apartment off of Fifth Avenue. It has two bedrooms (one is a guest room and sewing room) and an office, which is where she does all her writing.

Ann's apartment is decorated with classic good taste. Tan-and-white striped wallpaper covers the living room and dining room entry hallway. Rose-colored carpeting covers the floors. There are book-shelves in almost every room of Ann's apartment. They are filled with novels, biographies, nonfiction books, and children's books. Many of her own books sit on these shelves as well. Ann's apartment is furnished with simple but beautiful antiques. The living room is filled with comfortable couches and matching armchairs. A gallery of framed family photos lines the hallway.

Says Ann, "Anything that's handed down in the family becomes extremely important to me. There's a table that sits out on my enclosed porch — an old drop-leaf table with gatelegs — and I love it. I don't really have a spot for it in the apartment anymore, but I'll never get rid of it because it was my grandparents'. Maybe it was even my great-grandparents'!"

Ann's kitchen sports a number of cat magnets and a few *I Love Lucy* plates, which are only for show. In the office, the toys and joke items have started to get a little out of hand. There's a chicken that lays tiny plastic eggs, a collection of snow globes, and some tacky beach souvenirs. Ann enjoys a clean, orderly environment. Her apartment is always spotless.

Of course, a description of Ann's home would not be complete without introducing her two cats. Mouse is big and orange and has a quiet, mature personality. He loves to be petted, but he isn't a pest about it.

Rosie, also a male cat, is younger than Mouse.

A friend of Ann's found Rosie's mother abandoned and pregnant on a Brooklyn street. The friend took the mother in, let her give birth, then found homes for each kitten, as well as the mother. (Ann's former assistant, Bonnie, took the mama cat and one of the kittens. Their names are Stellar and Rubie.) Rosie is dark gray-and-white striped, and has the longest tail. He has grown to be quite big. He's much more skittish than Mouse. He lets only a few people other than Ann pet him. He likes to hide underneath chairs, and just stick out one paw or the tip of his tail. The cats are two of Ann's most beloved friends.

A few years ago, Ann embarked on a new and exciting adventure. She bought an old country house. It's on five and a half acres of wooded land. The house has pressed tin ceilings and orangy-red cypress wood beams. There are fourteen beautiful rooms that Ann furnished with antiques and copies of antiques. There's even a tower on top of the house. One room is the kids' guest room. It has rabbit print wallpaper and is filled with toys and kids' books. Ann turned the attic of the house into her office. It's huge — a good place to let her imagination spread out and wander.

At the house, Ann has been able to have her own garden again for the first time since she left her parents' house. She has a dozen different kinds of flowers, and there's the perfect, sunny spot in the back for her vegetable garden. Quail, pheasants, and wild turkeys crisscross the yard around the house.

Ann says, "I just wanted to have a place to get away from the city. I like being outdoors. I like the way the trees smell. I love New York, too. A lot of my friends are there, and there's always so much to do. But there's also so much traffic and dirt and crowding. The city is not peaceful, no matter what time of day, no matter how quiet it may seem. Not even at three in the morning."

It may be difficult to believe, but fame and success have their down sides as well. Ann must work

Ann on Being Successful

"I don't like being a celebrity. I don't like being in the spotlight. I never did. It bothers me that it matters to strangers who I am and what I do. Certainly it's very flattering, but if I had to choose between being a celebrity and not being one, I'd choose not to be one. I thank goodness people don't recognize me on the street. If they did, I don't know what I'd do. I'd feel such a lack of privacy.

"The foundation is the biggest positive aspect of my success. Having money doesn't matter much to me, except for two things — being able to give it away through the foundation and just being comfortable. I can remember eight or ten years ago lying in bed one morning and won-

cont.

dering if I'd be able to pay my electric bill that month. I'd figured things out to the penny, and an unexpected expense had come up. It's really nice not to have to worry about things like that now.

"If the Baby-sitters Club had never happened, I think I'd be doing what I did before I left Bantam — writing, and a lot of free-lance editing. That was fun, because my work was so varied.

"I don't think fame and wealth should be as important as they seem to be to so many people. I certainly never set out to be famous or wealthy. The kind of career I wanted when I was younger probably wouldn't have brought much of either one, because I wanted to be a teacher. So I don't think those things are important to me.

"Some people say that success equals money, but frankly, I don't think success is money at all. I think that's a very bad way of measuring it. Success is being the best at whatever you want to do well at. If you're a wonderful teacher, then you're a success, especially if that's what you wanted to be in the first place, if that was a goal you strived for and reached. I think it's too bad that people are called a success only if they're making a lot of money and their faces appear on the front of every magazine. That's only one kind of success."

extremely hard to keep up with the blinding pace of the Baby-sitters Club and Little Sister series. She doesn't get to write other books as often as she'd like. She has had to make many personal sacrifices in terms of free time, seeing friends, and being able to do things on the spur of the moment. She has created a rigid schedule for herself, and she cannot afford to miss a day of work. Not because she's sick. Not even because something else that's important comes up, like a personal problem.

Ann says, "If I could change one thing about my life, I'd have a less rigid work schedule. I don't mean less work to do, I mean fewer deadlines."

Fame can also be a little scary sometimes, especially if you're naturally shy, the way Ann is. One time, Ann had a speaking engagement at a public library in the Midwest. The time passed quickly. Then suddenly, Ann realized she was out of time, and had to wrap things up and hurry off to catch her plane home. She hadn't gotten a chance to sign autographs, and a number of the kids (and their parents) were disappointed.

So when Ann left, a few parents jumped in their cars and followed her to the airport. They weren't being nasty. In fact, they all said how much their children enjoyed her books and how excited the kids would be to get her autograph. But Ann felt frightened when they surrounded her and pushed pens and pieces of paper in her face. They weren't thinking about her. It was a real invasion of her privacy.

Being successful was hardest at first. Ann had

to adjust from living her quiet, concentrated life to being a part of a huge, public enterprise. Sometimes it was confusing when strangers wanted so much to become her friends. But over the past few years, she has grown more secure with her success. She probably won't ever be comfortable with large groups of people and strangers. But it's not nearly as scary as it once was.

In fact, Ann's job has forced her to deal with many things she might not have had to otherwise. For example, she has addressed audiences of over two thousand people. That's pretty impressive stuff for someone as shy as Ann.

But many of her closest friends stress that she's still the same old Ann. Kate says, "She hasn't really changed at all in terms of what's important to her and what she makes time for — her friends, her family, and the causes that she has supported. I think she has kind of surprised herself with how well she's been able to cope with her fame."

Says Ann, "I never expected half the things that have happened to me in my life. The Baby-sitters Club has been an incredible adventure. I'm just wondering what the next thirty-five years will bring!"

Happy reading to all BSC fans!

About the author

MARGOT BECKER R. was a dancer before she became an author. Her first adult novel was published when she was 23, and she used the money she earned from that book to go to West Africa and study dance. In addition to writing, she works at a community group in her Lower Manhattan neighborhood in New York City. She can often be found curled up with a book. Her most often asked question: What does the R stand for? Answer: Her mother's maiden name, which is Rubin.

THE BABY-SITTERS CLUB

by Ann M. Martin

Little Sister

by Ann M. Martin

Other books by
Ann M. Martin

Rachel Parker, Kindergarten Show-off
Eleven Kids, One Summer
Ma and Pa Dracula
Yours Turly, Shirley
Ten Kids, No Pets
Slam Book
Just a Summer Romance
Missing Since Monday
With You and Without You
Me and Katie (the Pest)
Stage Fright
Inside Out
Bummer Summer

Organizations mentioned in this book:

The Ann M. Martin Foundation
P. O. Box 1293
New York, NY 10011

Eden Institute Foundation, Inc.
One Logan Drive
Princeton, NJ 08540

The Fifty-Second Street Project
552 W. 52nd Street
New York, NY 10019

The Kopeyia Ghana School Fund, Inc.
1056 Oakland Court
Teaneck, NJ 07666

The Lisa Novak Community Libraries, Inc.
% Ann M. Martin
Scholastic Inc.
730 Broadway
New York, NY 10003

The Make-A-Wish Foundation of Metro
  New York, Inc.
382 Main Street
Port Washington, NY 11050

National Dance Institute
594 Broadway, Room 805
New York, NY 10012

The Princeton Small Animal Rescue League —
  S.A.V.E.
900 Herrontown Road
Princeton, NJ 08540

Save the Children
54 Wilton Road
P.O. Box 925
Westport, CT 06881

Starlight Foundation of Chicago
708 N. Dearborn
Chicago, IL 60610

THE BABY-SITTERS CLUB®

by Ann M. Martin

More titles... ▶

The Baby-sitters Club titles continued...

Available wherever you buy books...or use this order form.

Scholastic Inc., P.O. Box 7502, 2931 E. McCarty Street, Jefferson City, MO 65102

Please send me the books I have checked above. I am enclosing $_____
(please add $2.00 to cover shipping and handling). Send check or money order - no
cash or C.O.D.s please.

Name _____

Address _____

City_____ State/Zip_____

Tell us your birth date! _____

Please allow four to six weeks for delivery. Offer good in the U.S. only. Sorry, mail orders are not
available to residents of Canada. Prices subject to change.   BSC792

LITTLE 🍎 APPLE®

BABY-SITTERS

Little Sister™

by Ann M. Martin, author of *The Baby-sitters Club* ®

More Titles... ➡